JOURNEYS IN GREEN PLACES

JOURNEYS IN GREEN PLACES

THE SHORES AND WOODS OF WISCONSIN'S DOOR PENINSULA

Virginia S. Eifert

With Drawings by the Author

Wm Caxton Ltd
Sister Bay, Wisconsin
Evanston, Illinois

Copyright 1963 by Virginia S. Eifert, copyright 1989 by Larry Eifert, revised edition.

This edition published by Wm Caxton Ltd, Box 709, Sister Bay, WI 54234

First published 1963 by Dodd, Mead & Company, New York.

All rights reserved. No part of this book may be reproduced in any form or by any means without permission in writing from the publisher, except by a reviewer, who may quote brief passages in a review.

Printed in the United States of America

10   9   8   7   6   5   4   3   2   1

Library of Congress Cataloging in Publication Data

Eifert, Virginia Louise Snider, 1911-1966
    Journeys in green places: the shores and woods of Wisconsin's Door peninsula / by Virginia S. Eifert.
        p.   cm.
    Includes bibliographical references and index.
    ISBN 0-940473-13-5 : $20.00. – ISBN 0-940473-12-7 (pbk.) : $9.95
    1. Natural History – Wisconsin – Door County. I. Title.
QH105.W6E5   1989
508.775'63--dc20   89-17428
                                                                                   CIP

ISBN#   0-940473-12-7 paperback
              0-940473-13-5 hardcover

This book is affectionately dedicated
to
Mertha Fulkerson, Emma Toft
and the Ridges Association,
guardians of that ancient haunt of
boreal plants,
THE RIDGES

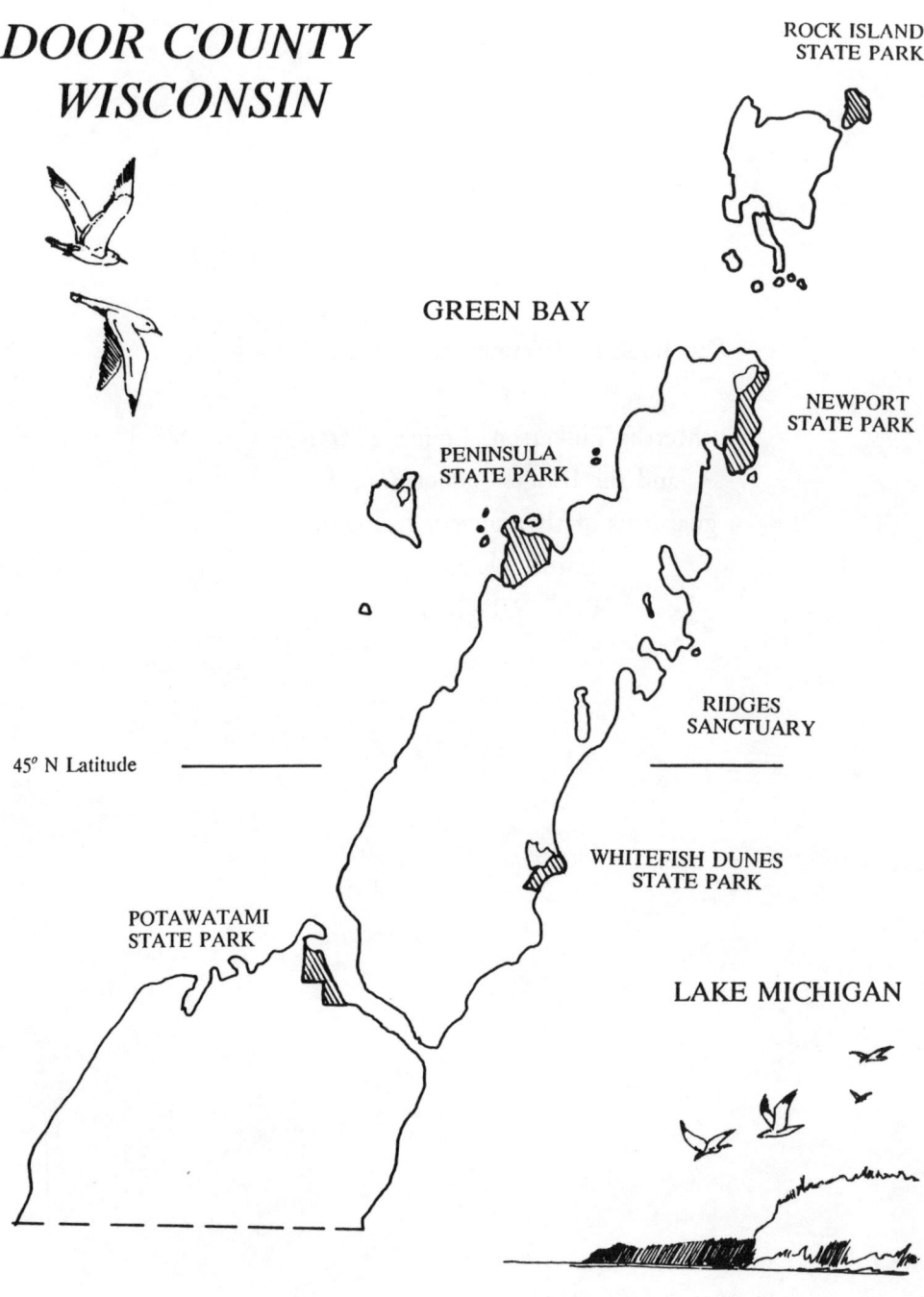

CONTENTS

INTRODUCTION		xi
1.	THE BEGINNINGS	1
2.	THE PENINSULA	18
3.	THE RIDGES	30
4.	THE PINE DUNES	54
5.	THE BOG	74
6.	ADVENTURES WITH ORCHIDS	100
7.	THE CONIFEROUS FOREST	115
8.	THE DECIDUOUS WOODS	136
9.	WATER GARDENS	162
10.	THE ALCHEMY OF AUTUMN	180
11.	THE ANATOMY OF NATURE	200
	BIBLIOGRAPHY	217
	INDEX	219

INTRODUCTION

TO find the unexpected in a world of the expected, to come upon a secluded corner of the past maintaining itself with an exquisite obedience to old laws, to know the sound of lake waves, the sweep of wind, the brilliance of sky, the calling of birds, is to open a door to a peculiar sense of awareness and fulfillment. To find all this in a water-rimmed area is an added pleasure, for there is a keen delight in bodies of land which are almost or entirely circled by water. Thoreau knew this feeling of intimacy with his surroundings when he said: "I have, as it were, my own sun and moon and stars, and a little world all to myself."

On an island one knows his boundaries; knows that if he follows any road, it will take him to the edge of his immediate world. This situation is found in the Door peninsula of Wisconsin—a narrow, tapering, ninety-miles-long finger of limestone and sand thrusting into northern Lake Michigan between the lake itself and Green Bay. The upper half of the peninsula, once only to be reached by sailing vessel, actually became an island when the ship canal was cut through at Sturgeon Bay. Thus, in crossing the bridge one comes into a separate landscape of rolling hills, bluffs, dunes, beaches, woods, fishing villages, resorts, harbors, and cherry orchards.

It is the world of an island isolated in its waters, a place where the story of the past is evident in the ecology of an area, a place where

INTRODUCTION

the customs of the past are still evident in some of its people and communities. It is an old land, discovered by white men long before the rest of the upper Great Lakes country was known. In 1634, Jean Nicolet came to the place on this peninsula called the Red Banks, expecting to have reached China, but finding instead a large encampment of Winnebagoes. Men have been coming here ever since. Belgians, Danes, and Germans settled the lower parts of Door County, Scandinavians and Moravians the upper, and Icelanders made a little Iceland out of Washington Island which lies off the tip of the peninsula. In a stern and often harsh land of long winters and short summers, they found much of the same challenge to life which they had known and accepted in their native countries.

Some say that Door County, Wisconsin, is like New England; however, the people are staunch defenders of their peninsula's uniqueness. They say that it is like no other place in America: "New England is all very well, but Door County is Door County, and the two are very different." Yet, the rugged similarities are there. The peninsula has the turbulent lake instead of the sea, and although the stone is not granite, the shore is much the same sort of gnarled, rockbound coast typical of New England.

That sturdy, no-compromise quality of the people and the land is also found in the trees, flowers, and lichens which, in spite of hardship which might discourage and destroy many other plants, grow in Door County.

To come to the peninsula means to drive, for there are no railroads and no large air fields. Therefore, the visitor must come for the sake of the peninsula alone, not just because it happens to be on the route to someplace else. It is a dead-end destination.

Mid-way up the peninsula, Sturgeon Bay, lying on both sides of the ship canal, forms the meeting place for the two highways coming up from the south and leading into the peninsula. The waterway and harbor are busy. Gulls are everywhere, the big lake freighters in the shipyard loom tall, and fishing boats and yachts line the shores. Across the bridge, the two roads climb together to a broad, hilly

INTRODUCTION

view which, in springtime, is white with miles of cherry blossoms. The left-hand fork takes to the hills, while the right-hand fork follows the lake shore. The hill-road skirts Green Bay, now high, now dipping into the hollows beside the water. Each hollow holds a harbor and a village with white houses, fish nets drying on reels, and snowy gulls lined up on the weathered gray sheds, hopefully waiting for the fishing boats to come in with the day's catch. Egg Harbor, Fish Creek, Ephraim, and Sister Bay are each set about five miles apart.

Out of Sister Bay the apple and cherry orchards border the road, then end abruptly at a sudden and splendid view of a distant headland. It is white-based where waves cream on white rocks far below, the waters of the bay very blue-purple or misty gray, with perhaps a wisp of dark smoke from a freighter on the horizon. A swoop down, and the road comes quickly into and out of the village of Ellison Bay.

To the left on the Garrett Bay road, not far from the village, lies the Clearing, 135 acres of woodland and meadow on the high limestone bluffs above Green Bay. It is an adult vacation school in the woods, a philosophic venture in teaching which was begun in 1935 by the late landscape architect, Jens Jensen. He named it for a certain clearing of the mind which he hoped would take place in all who came; for man, he felt, sorely needed to renew himself by contact with nature. The Clearing is now operated by the Wisconsin Farm Bureau. There are week-long classes which vary from nature, to music, to art, to literature, to philosophy, to agronomy, to writing.

The highway has only another scant five miles to go before reaching the jumping-off place at Gill's Rock and the Washington Island ferry landing. This is the end of the peninsula and the end of the road.

Beyond here, the straits of the Door of Death rushing past the blunted tip of the peninsula's forested headlands have always presented a menace to men and boats, and many have been lost. More

INTRODUCTION

than two hundred Potawatomies coming from the island perished here in a storm. La Salle's ship, the *Griffin*, loaded with furs from Washington Island and sailing off to an unknown fate, may have sunk in the straits. Numerous shipwrecks lie in the Door of Death—Porte des Morts, the French called it.

About thirteen miles south of Sister Bay, on the road which followed the Lake Michigan shore out of Sturgeon Bay, there is the old village of Bailey's Harbor, whose history has always been bound up in the vicissitudes of the lake. A view of a shining bay reveals a far shore curving like a silver half-moon to the east. Around this bay there lies a dramatically different landscape, different from anything else on the peninsula and strangely reminiscent of the remote wilderness of spruce bogs of the Boreal Zone and the subarctic. This is a magical area, holding many botanical treasures which are protected as part of the Ridges Sanctuary. Its ecological story and its splendid wild flowers bring naturalists and botanists from many parts of the world.

Although a visit at any time is rewarding in this place of ancient lineage, the most beautiful and doubtless most flower-filled period begins in mid-May when the arbutus, early orchids and dwarf irises bloom at the same time as the orchards on the peninsula. In June the greatest number of orchids may be found.

When the cherries are ripe in late July, the Ridges begins another burst of bloom which puts hundreds of bog-stars, the white parnassias, and dancing blue harebells in the sunny areas, pyrolas and Indian pipe in the shade, and the tall, purple-fringed orchid in damp, sandy places, to be followed by fringed gentians in September. Autumn, usually coming later on the peninsula than in northern Wisconsin's upper mainland, is usually at its best in mid-October. Snow may come before the colors are gone, but not until later will the bay freeze and the snow pile softly and silently over all the

INTRODUCTION

evergreen plants in the Ridges, leaving only the ragged spruces and the tall pines standing above the drifts.

This book is intended not only as an exploration of that special landscape of the Ridges, but as an aid to appreciating the ecology of the northern United States and Canada, all of which were similarly influenced by the ravages and rebirth brought about by the Ice Age. It is intended as a guide book not only to that fascinating living museum of plants and atmosphere bequeathed by the Glacial Era and illustrated so vividly in the Door peninsula, particularly in the Ridges, but also as a key to an understanding of the year, with its subtle overtones of the Ice Age which are still visible in the changing pattern of the seasons.

CHAPTER ONE

THE BEGINNINGS

AFTER last night's spring storm, the wind was still raging across the lake. Waves broke and creamed over a reef, came pounding in toward the shore, and then, losing strength, curled foaming on the beach. The spent water, carrying froth, ran in on the wet sand. A single gull, white against the blue, seemed to be almost translucent in the brilliance and clarity of the sunlight. Except for the flying bird, I might have stood alone at the rim of creation, with only the water, the sky, and the sand as elements out of which might develop the world of plants and animals. Behind me, in sand and earth and wet swales and swamps and forests, lay the details of the story of how these three factors accomplished that great populating of the land.

Here lay the story of the plant successions as they took place in the past ten thousand years after the last glacial ice melted. Here I might try to understand how the barren, chill land and waters across the top of North America had set about the long and wonderful task of planting themselves anew.

Nature, seeming to abhor a bare place, has a varied selection of upholsterings immediately at hand to cover any vacancy and need. There is a plant to fit almost every situation and every sort of poverty and wealth; nature has the plant for the occasion. Others are evidently kept in stock to fit a changing haunt after the original cover has served its usefulness and must be succeeded by something more elaborate. Plants are continually moving across the face of the earth. Animals, geared to live wherever plants do, adapt their own means of life to the changing of the vegetation.

An old legend in the Philippines tells of a time when there was neither life nor land in the world—only the sea, and the sky, and a flying bird. And when the bird at last grew weary of always being on the wing, it provoked a quarrel between the sky and the sea. The winds raged, and the sea threw great angry blue-green combers and stinging spray so high that they slashed against the sky itself. And the sky, infuriated, boiled into a rage of violent tempests which hurled down heavy thunderings. The thunder solidified as it tumbled into the sea and was changed into rocks. And as the rocks piled up and up, finally reaching the surface, there was land at last—there were islands—there was a place on which a bird might come down to rest its wings.

The water, the sky, the sand, and life—both in legend and in truth—these are the essence of the beginnings of the world. They were also the vital factors which went into action at the time the Ice Age ended, when life had to come back quickly into the lately frozen and devastated areas.

Nature with proper ingredients responds to situations in orderly plans and with plants that follow in sequence to create more complex designs. They are patterns and plans which worked well, millions of years ago, during the earliest populating of the earth, when evolution required a tremendous amount of time to accomplish its

THE BEGINNINGS

ends by means of developing the perfect answers for given problems.

Those basic beginnings of getting plants to grow on sand and rock and of creating soil for them still take place in the same orderly manner and sequence. The bare and wind-blown beach behind me, where on this spring day the wind was drying the top grains of sand after the night's rain and moving them along in a fine sandblasting, was not ready for trees or wild roses or ferns or orchids. Transplanted here by some misguided gardener, they would have quickly perished. A long, deliberate passage of time and change must take place before there can be soil and woods, or meadows and marshes, instead of the open sand and the barren rock. Nature, the all-powerful, can do it. Nature, the all-powerful, has been doing it for hundreds of millions of years and is doing it today.

But it had happened in this place behind me on this shore during the past seven to eight thousand years. The same procedure had taken place within the past ten to eleven thousand years as far south as the Ohio River, and in very much less time in Canada. But it had all been virtually the same sequence.

Such puny measurements of time are as nothing to nature, which has had eons in which to work and experiment and is in no hurry at all. Because nature's usually large-scale operations are far more difficult for human beings to comprehend, I need to come to this place on a Wisconsin peninsula thrusting into upper Lake Michigan to find a more concise narration of the greater story. I find it one of the most vivid examples of plant successions. It is a picture book complete with text. And if I can understand the pictures and read the text, then I shall know pretty much of what happened all across North America when the Ice Age ended. It is a small place in which to tell so grand a story—so world-wide a story—yet its very compactness here may bring a better understanding than the whole tremendous scope of the same tale as expressed across a continent or around the world.

JOURNEYS IN GREEN PLACES

THE CHARA

The wind blew, and a wave broke a little closer and splashed on my shoes. The gull flew and squeaked in the spring sunshine, the water glittered so that I could scarcely open my eyes, and the sand took the undulating imprint of another wave as sand has been taking wave imprints almost since the beginning of the world.

A fragile-looking roll of bleached floss lay at the rim of the storm beach where last week's tempest had thrown it when the waves were higher. The floss crumbled in my fingers and left on them a whitish residue, like an exceedingly fine sand. But it was not sand. It was silica and calcium carbonate, and the floss was composed of dead

Chara

chara (kā́ra)* plants, one of the green algae and a very complex one. The individual plants rolled up in the storm-tossed bundle were eight inches long, or a little more or less. They were very slender and composed of innumerable whorls of tenuous branches which tapered to smaller ones around the tips. In my fingers they crumbled like infinitely fine and fragile fish bones. In life they would have been dark green and resilient, like grass; they would have possessed a strong smell.

For so primitive a plant the reproduction of chara is highly complicated, and has been both a marvel and a puzzle to botanists. In addition, chara is able to take calcium carbonate from water in the limestone regions in which it grows, and precipitate it as a fine

---

* See index, under common names, for botanical names of plants which appear in the following pages.

powder, simply by giving off the plant's own carbon dioxide. In also taking silica from these waters, chara thus acquires a grittiness of form which is far different from the usually soft, yielding, and easily disintegrated algae.

The mineral and chemical content of chara is left on the lake bottom when the plant dies, and with the accumulation of these decaying and decayed plants over thousands of years, the extensive beds of sediment in the lake form a soft limestone material which never hardens, called marl. In building up the lake bottom it becomes one of the steps toward the attainment of dry land. In my hands that morning I held plants shaped in the dawn of creation, and in this white stuff on my fingers I knew the material which had laid some of the foundations of lake and shore and forest.

For I had begun to realize that I could not know of today or understand what I found in the wild without first finding out all I could about the long-gone yesterdays, back to the beginnings. Instead of finding only a chaotic, temporary arrangement of plants and animals and their reactions to situations in which everything might seem to come and go as if in a static landscape, I recognized some of the real meanings in their associations with each other. There is a marvelous and inescapable plan by which this plant is found here and that animal there, and certain ones are always found together. Part of the plan puts the waves and the chara at my feet, puts certain trailing and rooting plants to holding the sand a little distance back from where I stood—part of the same plan which gave me a distant skyline of spruces and a rim of pine crowns, far beyond the restless sands where neither would grow. It gave me the root-anchored dunes and the place where the sand itself was finally concealed beneath a carpet of creeping boreal plants.

SEAWATER AND LIMESTONE

Limestone cliffs stand about a mile inland from this sand shore. Long ago they marked a terminus of the oldest beach when the lake water was very high and lapped its rocks. Some of the rock ledges, however, in other places slope to the present edge of the water, around the curves of the bay, disappear in the depths of the lake, and do not emerge again until they rise between Georgian Bay and Lake Huron to form the Saugeen Peninsula of Ontario. These rocks are of whitish Niagara limestone which was formed during the Silurian period, between three hundred and fifty and four hundred million years ago. At the water's rim were ledges in which fossil coral colonies still remained in the place where the corals lived when the inland sea water receded after covering much of the interior of North America. The great deposition of corals and limestone ended around three hundred and fifty million years ago. Yet as I stood on those ancient animal remains, there seemed to be no gap, suddenly, between their lives and mine.

The Silurian seas had spread warm salt water over a large portion of the continent, especially across the middle west, the north, and the east. Calcium carbonate was in the water in which lived billions of creatures whose bodies utilized the calcium carbonate to form shells. Some of the creatures were huge—as the cephalopods which were rather like octopuses six feet long, living in heavy shell cornucopias, and others which dwelt in shells as big as wagon wheels. The majority, however, were small to microscopic, multiplying, living, dying in incredible quantities, and for millions of years adding to the sediment on the bottom.

When these creatures died—the brachiopods, trilobites, corals, crinoids, clams, snails, foraminifera, cephalopods—their shells precipitated to the floor of the sea. The lower layers of this whitish lime sediment, hardened by time, pressure, and heat, formed limestone at the rate of an inch in several thousand years. The limestone eventually lay hundreds of feet thick on top of the ancient granites which, with basalt, formed the original surface of the earth before the oceans came, long before life appeared and sediment hardened. This same kind of limestone forms the lip of Niagara Falls, and because it was first discovered there, it now bears that name. In the Great Lakes region its layers are between two hundred and four hundred and fifty feet thick.

The Silurian seas drew back and disappeared at last. The limestone either sank or in places was elevated. The seas were followed by the period of swamps and coal-making forests, and eons of change went by. Earth formed, forests grew. Rivers developed a slow chiseling of water-courses, draining and changing the landscape, slowly cutting valleys which deepened and broadened. Rivers chewed through the rock itself—through limestone and sandstone and shale and quartzite and granite. There were no Great Lakes then. They would later occupy some of those old, worn, gentle river valleys.

THE ICE

Eleven thousand years ago something remarkable was happening to the world. It was felt in the sea and on the land and in the atmosphere itself. What happened then is the key to the explanation of landscape and soil, of plants and animals, even people. It was eleven thousand years ago that the Ice Age ended.

It would take thousands of years before the great ice itself had all finally melted away, shrunk to its lair in the Arctic, but the vital fact was that eleven thousand years ago the ice was no longer advancing. It was at last melting gloriously and leaving a wet and ravaged land open for the return of plants and animals which were already following closely in its wake. Life, for so long pushed into a comparatively small area in the south, was bursting at the seams. Its population explosion required elbow room and breathing space. As quickly as the ice went away, plants and animals were moving into the old haunts of the glacier.

Eleven thousand years ago, a certain mark was left on land and in the sea. At that turning point, the Arctic Ocean evidently froze over, and because of this, the heavy snowfalls in the Arctic ended for lack of that ocean's open water to supply the great precipitation. No more cold water came circulating frigidly out of the Arctic Ocean into the Atlantic, chilling it and its surroundings. These facts were only recently found in the core drillings which were made in the Atlantic Ocean floor by expeditions sent out by Lamont Geological Laboratory at Columbia University. Far down was found a gray layer of sediment left by creatures living in cold waters, while just above, in a sharp line of demarcation, there began a pinkish sediment characteristic of life in warmer waters. When radiocarbon tests were made on the top layer of the gray sediment, just where the pink began, it was found to be dated at eleven thousand years ago. This date was evidently one of the most important in the entire northern hemisphere because of the way in which it coincided with significant events in the Arctic.

Eleven thousand years ago, early Stone Age men who had been living around the shores of the Arctic Ocean started a sudden migration southward into warmer parts. The freezing of the ocean had shut off their food supply.

The Ice Age, of course, may not have truly and totally ended, for this period in which we live is believed to be just another long interglacial period, as occurred several other times during the Ice Age itself. It is predicted that the glaciers may return when once more the Arctic Ocean is free of ice—and each year it is known and recorded with certainty that that ice is growing less. But at least that moment, eleven thousand years ago, marked a certain vital turning point in terms of human history and the natural history of the Northern Hemisphere.

The Ice Age had begun about a million years ago. This was only a morsel of time as compared with the great geologic eras before that and what happened during their long, long periods. But this comparatively short Age of Ice was the one which perhaps had the greatest effect upon our own lives and on our surroundings. Human beings had evolved during this era and were tremendously influenced by the progression of the Ice Age in Europe, Asia, and America.

There may have been other prolonged periods of cold in the earth's history, but any record of them has been largely lost under the rock layers which formed at later times. We know that in the

THE BEGINNINGS

Cretaceous period, one hundred and thirty million years ago, the continent was warmed with a gentle climate extending all the way to what is now the Arctic. The evidence of this is found in fossil remains of palm trees, figs, magnolias, and bald cypresses which grew nearly all the way to the Arctic Circle. The continent was largely covered with a magnificent forest composed of some of the finest trees the world had perhaps ever known, and the majority were of species which we have today—sycamore, beech, oak, maple, tulip, sassafras, gum, poplar, willow, maple, the coniferous trees, and many more.

The beginning of climatic change between the north and south and a certain cooling must have begun in a much later period, the Pliocene. Probably by the end of that period the Ice Age itself had in fact begun. New finds in core drillings have uncovered fossil remains of beautiful, minute, star-shaped creatures which may have been either plant or animal, or akin to both, called discoasters. They were tremendously abundant in plankton during the Pliocene, and then very suddenly became extinct about a million years ago when the seas cooled and the Ice Age began. Not until very recently, when the discoasters were found in the sediment, was a really accurate date obtainable for the beginning of the Glacial Era.

No one as yet has found a totally acceptable theory of why it all happened. There can be so many explanations, each one logical enough yet readily to be supplanted by some other equally reasonable theory. One theory is that because of a migration of poles caused by a shifting of the earth's crust, the North Pole was located in the Pacific Ocean. Those great wet areas would not freeze, and cold would lose its impact. But when the Pole shifted to its present location over land, the lowered temperatures evidently caused a tremendous amount of precipitation in the form of snow.

The great snowfall of the world thus must have begun at the end of the Pliocene—when the waters chilled, and the beautiful little geometric discoasters all died—and it snowed, and it snowed, and it snowed. At first, perhaps, it was no more than one severe winter after another. Annual seasonal changes might have ended the snows for a time, yet brought back shorter and shorter greening and growing periods. As more and more snow fell in the north and piled up, the general temperature of the whole year grew cooler. Great and strange changes began to take place from the north to the south.

When the snow failed to melt (or, when it did, simply was changed to ice), the very pressure of flake upon flake began to alter the lower layers to make an icy snow called névé. The névé then became compressed into glacier ice. The procedure took place by the same basic method by which a boy packs snow to make an ice ball. Pressure and a little melting will do it, will change snow into ice, and, in the case of the vast snow fields of the far north, change it into glacier ice which has the power of motion.

By the time when there were no real summers, but only incessant winter or near-winter in a damp, chill, snowy climate, the growing weight of the snow on top of the ice caused the latter to be squeezed out. It was as if a mass of firm dough on a breadboard, pushed down with the palm of the hand, was squeezed out on all sides. So, as the great ice was pressed down, it began to move. It started in the only direction in which it could go—south around the top of the world, south of the polar ice cap.

Now and again, warming trends caused the advancing ice to melt along its edges, and for a time it might then have become considerably less. Yet the melting seldom lasted long enough to halt the glacier, and for thousands of years it grew and thickened and slowly spread until it was two miles deep. It was a great advancing cliff of blue-white ice, discolored by dust and debris blown against its face by southerly winds, ice that was floored with dead trees, rocks, sand, gravel, and earth which it had caught up in itself as it spread and advanced, and which were being dragged along with it. Wherever the ice cliffs paused for a while and melted, some of this debris was dropped, then perhaps was carried on again to the very southernmost rim of the advance of the ice.

THE BEGINNINGS

In a million years there were four separate great glaciers in North America. Each one had an existence of many thousands of years before melting vastly and drawing back to leave a mild interglacial period in which life could return, before the ice once more advanced and again ruined everything. This process of glaciation was so slow that it was possible for generations of plants and animals to live and die in its shadow, never having to move out of the way. A tree standing three feet away from the edge of the wall of ice might still be there a hundred years later, while the ice mass might have come only an inch or two closer. But it was coming, coming inexorably, and everything that was in its way either had to escape or be engulfed at last.

The tree could not escape, but it could send its annual crop of seeds out of the way. The predominating winds must have been northern and northwesterly. They blew the seeds a little distance to the south and southeast, far enough for the seedlings to grow, have time to mature, and send their own seeds a little distance south. It was far enough. Generation after generation of trees and flowers thus lived below the glacier, sent its progeny farther and farther away, until they were safe from the ice's immediate menace, while the older trees and flowers had been long since crushed beneath the glacier.

The whole climate of America and much of its landscape was altered. The effect of the cooling and the great drainage of the melting was felt all the way to the Gulf of Mexico. During the peak of the Ice Age when so much of the world's precipitation was locked up in the great ice cap around the northern parts of the earth, there was a great lowering of the oceans. Shorelines of the world were thus considerably lessened, on the average lying two hundred feet below where they are today.

Eventually, as the Canadian forests were completely engulfed, trees and flowers which once had lived in Canada now extended hundreds of miles south across what is now Illinois, Indiana, Ohio, and Pennsylvania, while the hardwood forests were concentrated in the Carolinas, Tennessee, and Alabama. The entire north was ruined. It lay under an inconceivably great weight of ice that was five to ten thousand feet thick.

This great weight alone was enough to have changed any landscape. It caused bedrock to sink, and it deepened the valleys of old rivers. It squeezed molten rock up around the present shores of Lake Superior. The movement of the juggernaut, slow as it was, with the tremendous abrasive power of boulders and gravel caught up in its lower parts, had a gigantic sandpapering action. The harrow teeth of the glacier carved channels in the bedrock, smoothed the hills, polished off the bones of mountains, and totally altered both the landscape and its drainage systems.

For as it pushed south, like the giant bulldozer that it was, it was shoving masses of sand and gravel ahead of its course. This material dammed rivers and forced them elsewhere. It shunted the Ohio and Missouri rivers to the routes they now take, and it changed the route of the Mississippi. In melting, the ice left huge sand and gravel dumps to make moraine hills and other ice-created prominences, or filled hollows with glacial debris. Buried masses of ice were left behind to become thousands of northern lakes. They and the long scratches on rock, as well as casually deposited boulders brought down from Canada, are today unmistakable signatures of glaciation.

The four major ice sheets each covered a somewhat different terrain. The final one, the Wisconsin, extended farthest south. The total glaciation might be said to have in general covered the northeast all the way down to Cape Cod, Boston, and New York. Over the rest of the continent its southern limit extended along the present course of the Ohio River to the foot of Illinois, then followed the route of the Missouri River, crossed the Rockies to Seattle, and reached up the west coast into Alaska. For an unfathomed reason, all four ice sheets missed covering and grinding off certain isolated spots in Wisconsin and Illinois.

And so the ice came, and the ice went. The landscape and the

THE BEGINNINGS

life it left behind are the landscape and life we know today in the northern states and Canada.

THE RETURN

When at last the ice was melting in great floods of water that poured down the valleys and rivers into the Mississippi and the St. Lawrence, and warm, drying breezes from the south replaced the chill, wet winds off the ice cliffs, life must have come back in a hurry. Everything had been so concentrated in such a compressed area in the south that the desperate overcrowding and the difficulty in finding food must have sent creatures on foot or on wing, along with seeds on the winds, back into the north where open, empty areas were being left in the great thaw. Birds must have begun an annual cycle of migration in the interglacial periods, for the cycle of the seasons persisted in bringing a return of winter, and with it both a shortening of food supplies and an uncomfortable chill.

The return of plant life to the American north was unhindered. Our major mountain ranges lay north and south, but in Europe it was a different matter. There, with the ranges lying generally east and west, much plant life became extinct because it could not escape from the glaciers.

In its melting, the ice only momentarily left a vacant landscape. As fast as it was open, nature set about to occupy it. In the north it was filled with innumerable ice-water lakes, large and small, with rapid, overly-full streams running over glacier-dropped boulders; with gravel, sand, and loess hills, all bare and wet and chill, all without life. Scratched bedrock and whole mountainsides, scraped as clean as the bald heads of giants, waited for a decent covering of lichens and mosses and for the other plants which would follow these pioneers.

On southerly winds, the plants came north. Kind by kind, as they had slowly moved south, so now, with perhaps much greater speed and urgency, they returned. The northern flora which in some instances had had to go almost as far as the Gulf of Mexico, followed a cool, damp climate which was now extending itself ever farther to the north.

This, not the new heat of the south, was what they required for life—each plant has its own physical needs for warmth or cold—and so they accompanied their preferred climate back to the north. Here and there, however, far south, in isolated pockets, some of the northern plants remained as fragments in a post-glacial landscape. The pine lands of Louisiana still have partridgeberries which are left over from those times. In Kentucky and Tennessee I have found arbutus, wintergreen, and other northerners on high places with the spruce and hemlock; in Pennsylvania, New Jersey, Rhode Island, and North Carolina there are cranberry-spruce-tamarack bogs remaining in a much different sort of surrounding terrain than is their normal habitat in the north. In Illinois and Indiana there are isolated corners of tamarack bog, white pine, and related plants, surviving in a landscape where oak woods, prairies, and mile-long cornfields have long since prevailed.

Deep well-drillings today bring up peat containing pollen grains from plants which had lived far southward during the glacial and interglacial periods—the swamp spruce, aspen, tamarack, and balsam fir. These have all been gone long since and are now native five hundred miles and more due north.

In some parts of a once ice-covered world, the primary stage of sequences in the return of plants had to begin with the tundra. This low growth of small flowers, grasses, sedges, dwarf willows, and birches only a few inches tall could live in a stern climate and in a sterile, stony, acid, cold gravel. As the tundra continued northward on the heels of the ice, it was quickly followed by the formation of peat bogs into which finally came tamarack and swamp spruce. Then, in the warming, drying landscape immediately behind, came the spruce-fir and the pine-hemlock forests, or the beech-maple or oak-hickory forest climax. They all came in an orderly sequence, as

THE BEGINNINGS

each zone continued to move north in following its chosen kind of climate and landscape.

The vast spruce-fir forest of the Boreal Zone finally lay where it does now, stretching all the way across Canada and in only a few places dipping into the United States—in upper New England and Maine, in upper Michigan, Wisconsin, and Minnesota, and in the high mountains of the west. The tundra had traveled to the spartan climate where it now lives in the subarctic beyond the spruce bogs, and up to the line of perpetual snow in the Arctic. In the United States, an alpine tundra is found today only above the timber line on the tops of the Rocky Mountains and on such heights as Mount Washington in New Hampshire.

The deciduous forests came with the drying and warming period; a sudden hot and dry spell in the middle west about two thousand years ago evidently ended the sojourn of most of the plants of a cool, damp climate below the Great Lakes. Instead, the midwest became a country of oak-hickory forests, mixed deciduous woods, and wet prairie. The latter formed as the great shallow lakes and subsequent marshes which had been left by melt-water had dried in the hot wind.

Where did they all come from, exactly, the plants which so quickly seemed to repopulate the devastated area once occupied by the great ice? The uncovered ground around the Great Lakes is believed to have obtained plants from at least three different centers of life—from the Rio Grande valley and the arid southwest, from the southeastern forests, and from the Atlantic coastal plain. Along the Great Lakes many animals and plants are similar to those along the Atlantic coast; the deciduous trees are much like those in the southern Appalachians; and there are cacti, black-eyed Susans, silphiums, rattlesnakes, and pocket gophers which all came from the southwest.

The great glory of the returning forests and their wild flowers stemmed from the tremendous wilderness in the Smoky Mountains of eastern Tennessee—the beeches, basswoods, and maples which brought with them the trilliums, hepaticas, violets, and many other spring flowers. The bald cypresses, which once had lived almost all the way to the Arctic Circle, together with some of the more southern and subtropical plants like the papaw, persimmon, resurrection fern, sweet-bay magnolia, spider lily, lotus, and giant cane, came back only as far north as southern Illinois and Indiana.

The beach grasses, sea rocket, and beach pea on the Lake Michigan shore are descendants of those which migrated here from the dunes along the Atlantic coast. The pitcher plant in the bogs traveled a great distance to where it is now abundant. It evidently originated as a tropical plant in the Gulf states where some of its kin remain, yet must have found a vacant space in the sphagnum bog association as it moved north in the changing climatic sequence. The pitcher plant literally hopped aboard, and has long since been acclimated to the rigors of the north country, and to the demanding, restricted territory of the acid bog.

To look across this placid, sunny landscape of America, which once lay two miles deep under ice, to see the woods, the prairie, the marsh, the bog, the shore, and to know that every single plant in all this serene country came here originally from somewhere else is to begin to realize the enormousness of what nature was confronted with when the Ice Age ended, when the great springtime began, and when thousands of square miles of wet country waited to be replanted.

THE PLANTING

It must have been one of the most gigantic, most rapid, and wide-scale plowing-and-planting operations in the world's entire history, for perhaps never before had so large an area (in America, Europe, and Asia simultaneously) needed such fast attention. Nature could not wait. The land could not wait. All that bare sand and gravel and earth had to be fastened down as quickly as possible before it was further altered by every rain and wind, before all the rock powder and minerals were carried away and deposited in the oceans.

THE BEGINNINGS

That haze of green was being drawn quickly over the raw earth in the wake of the retreating ice.

Boreal botany came on the heels of the ice, was most characteristic of the Glacial Period, coming as it did at the beginning of the replanting. It was the most immediate and vital part of the colonizing and planting in the difficult, often cruel and fluctuating circumstances of land below the ice. Boreal plants are still pioneers today, are the damp, cool buffer between the subarctic and the temperate United States. They are a constant reminder of that not-so-distant past.

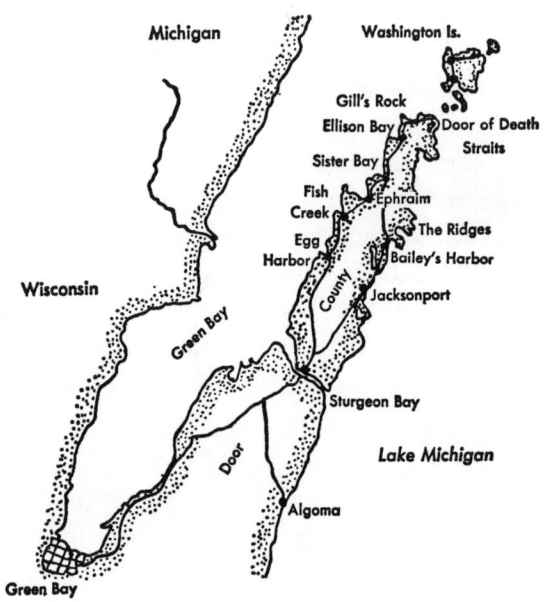

CHAPTER TWO

THE PENINSULA

AT the close of the Ice Age, melt-water filled the great hollows which used to be old river valleys. They had been gouged and deepened and enlarged by the ice, and now the melt-off filled them and created the Great Lakes. The water at first extended very much farther than the present-day expanses of the five lakes, and no doubt the Wisconsin peninsula was under water for a long time during the great melting, overflowing, and draining period.

The Door Peninsula is a long, narrow, limestone promontory, part of the old Niagara escarpment. It stands like a rim of a saucer at this point, the rest of it passing like the lower dip of the saucer quite beneath Lake Michigan and the state itself, to emerge farther east as the peninsula in Lake Huron.

The Wisconsin peninsula is nearly ninety miles long, with the

THE PENINSULA

waters of Green Bay on the northwest and the open expanse of Lake Michigan on the southeast. The thumblike peninsula is only about twenty-two miles wide at its lower end, tapering to a tip of less than two miles in width where the dangerous Door of Death straits rip past its rocky headlands and stony beaches, with Washington Island and lesser islands jutting from the cold waters beyond the straits.

The peninsula and the islands were left standing after the tremendous weight of the glaciers caused a great sagging and sinking of the limestone beds around them, thus forming Green Bay and Lake Michigan itself. The unsinkable peninsula had been scoured off by a lobe of glacial ice filling Green Bay and by another lobe on the Lake Michigan side. Its top was further polished and scraped when a third ice lobe ground its way over the surface and took off everything that had once lived and grown there.

As the floor of the lake began to rise after the weight of the ice was removed, tilting somewhat to the south, the water drained down the rivers into the Mississippi, and the peninsula finally got its back above water. This is believed to have been about the time of the conclusion of the final push of ice which came into Lake Michigan almost as an afterthought of the Ice Age, between seven and eight thousand years ago. The Green Bay side of the peninsula was left with almost sheer limestone cliffs, carved into great headlands and indented with deep, circular bays. But on the Lake Michigan side, where the escarpment rocks slope into the lake, the shores were marked into a series of large, gentle, half-moon scallops, making bays which had low rocky shores and received much sand washing in from the south. On this side of the peninsula, therefore, broad beaches and, in places, high dunes were formed. Here also, in a certain beach area in a large bay with a special southeast exposure, something strange and wonderful happened and then forget to go away when similar places in this area and latitude became extinct.

Surely, at no place along any shoreline in the world, when the Ice Age ended, were the beach-levels to be found where they are now located. A great raising of the oceans had come at the same time as the lowering of the Great Lakes shorelines, and for the same reason. The great melting and drainage had been simply putting back into the seas some of that tremendous bulk of water which for so many thousands of years had been literally out of circulation, bound up in solid form in an ice cap two miles thick.

Therefore, I knew that the sand upon which I stood on a spring day had, less than a hundred years ago, been under water. The oldest and original shoreline and beach were now a mile or more away, inland at the base of the cliffs. As the lake had continued to drain, the shorelines had dropped successively, so that wherever a beach had once lain for many years, a ridge of wave-and-wind-pushed sand, a low dune, was left behind to mark the place, while the water now splashed some distance away, making still another beach and dune. The space lying between the base of the cliffs and the place where I now stood became ultimately occupied with one old beach after another. At least sixteen low ridges mark these sixteen old shorelines, each one separated from the other by a wet, low place—a bog, or swale, or swamp. Down in the lake even now the seventeenth ridge is forming, my assurance of the continuity to be found in the orderly processes of nature.

THE SAND

The sand! As the waves broke at my feet, I watched how the wind blew sand endlessly in a fine storm off the crest of the low dune behind me, a blurring of fine grains which caught among plants at a distance back from the storm beach. The sand! Where did it come from? The waves had brought it into this point; but sand is a restless thing, and it may have traveled half way around the world. Sand is a by-product, the end result of rock—granitic rock, quartz rock, or sandstone. Since there is only limestone on these shores, the sand must have come from far away.

Sand and stone are related one to the other. The stones on the shore bear the guise of permanence, and the sand seems ever to be on the move; yet they are still akin. There is always the illusion that

THE PENINSULA

the stones, of all things on earth, must stay—that rock surely must last forever. Yet change, even in rocks, is still the one permanent thing in nature. The stone is really no more permanent than the spring flower or the butterfly; yet the latter are geared to coming and going quickly, while the former knows the long, slow change which in the world of nature has no need for hurry. The tempo of nature is different in each creature and in each thing, but no creature or thing will stay forever without changing. Man may not last long enough to see some of these alterations; but they are there, moving inexorably on and on toward a future where change will still be the only stable and certain thing.

The igneous rocks were part of the beginnings of the world, and the sand has been reduced from some of those rocks, from the archaic mountains, probably that original range to the north of here whose roots are the worn-down Canadian Shield. Nature, making sand slowly, must begin with the disintegration of mountains. The action of cold and heat, of water entering cracks and inserting that potent leverage which breaks solid granite into fragments, of gravity rolling the pieces down slopes, caused whole mountain ranges eventually to wear away. Pieces carried by river water were smoothed and transported far off. They grew ever smaller, being broken again and again, until they finally attained their essential crystals to make the sand. No one can say where these rocks may have been before the sand itself lay with a deceiving quietude, lapped with water and bathed in sunshine, on a Great Lakes beach. The hypothesis is that the glaciers must have brought most of it here.

When the ice caught it up somewhere far to the north, the sand grains may have been sharp; but when they were left on the lake bottom and rolled and tumbled by the water, they became smoothed. The ice also brought granitic rocks of many kinds and left them here—chunks of mountains, fist-sized portions of archaic crystal—scattered upon the sand.

In itself, sand, except when it becomes sandstone, can be and must remain little more than sand, for on the open beach the wind moves it, grain by grain, breeze by breeze, year by year. Perhaps no grain of sand, when its habitat is the open beach, stays very long in one place. As waves come in they draw the grains back a little distance, push them forward on the next wave, leave them on the higher beach for the sun to dry and the wind to chase. The wind sweeping along the beach pushes the grains in a low, miniature sandstorm that blurs the distant view.

The open beach is patterned briefly with crow tracks and spider trails. It is littered with occasional fish skeletons well cleaned by the scavenging gulls and crows, with bluish crayfish nippers and broken carapaces, with a few bleached snail shells and a clam shell or two. The chara torn up from its submerged lake beds in storms and sent rolling in the waves is cast upon the beach at the outer reach of the spent waves. There the green plants bleach white, and the wind eventually rolls them someplace else where they are finally mashed and crumbled into the sand. Always the next wave, the next wind, the next storm will change the picture of the storm beach itself, this realm of the restless, this haunt of the homeless.

THE SAND PIONEERS

Only a few plants are equipped to be sand holders and can begin to halt the restless movement of the beach. These pioneers must endure the buffeting of wind and sand as well as the tremendous unsheltered glare, the reflected light, and the heat of the sun on the open desert of the beach. It is a situation which requires a great deal of adaptability and hardiness in plant or animal. Not many could last here for more than a few days. But sand pioneers are tough and strongly rooted. They are geared for just this sort of rugged environment, a place where plant competition is at a minimum, an area which is open to any newcomers which can stand the punishment. Some of these are the same species which inhabit similar areas of the sea coasts—the rye grass and marram grass. They grow in big solid tufts on the first low wave of dune, while on the more level sands grow the silvery rosettes of artemisia, the wormwood, sea rocket, beach pea, silvery cinquefoil, and colonies of the vital, pioneering beach rush.

THE SAND FENCE

The beach rush, one of the chief sand holders, is a magnificently successful plant in an uneasy habitat. As the seed of the rush sends out a single horizontal root, it puts up a thin, cylindrical shoot which is tough, resilient in the wind, too narrow and wiry to be touched or hurt by flying sand particles, too well insulated to be harmed by heat and excessive light. The single root and shoot multiply and, as the root extends itself, it is anchored with vertical roots going down to seek water, each horizontal node sending up another thin whiplash of a shoot. Finally, this evenly spaced procession of dark green stalks forms a straight line, with other lines striking off at right angles from the original rooting. The rushes make a sand fence. It is only a foot high or a little more, but serves the same purpose as the snow fence in winter or the fences placed upon restless dunes and sea beaches to stop the action of the sand. The blowing sand halts as it strikes this green barrier and drops behind it. Thus all along each traveling root-line there lies a small hummock of sand. At this point the beach has begun to come to rest.

It will be only a matter of time before other plants may grow behind the sand fence's protection, when the little dune becomes more stable and builds a larger dune. The heavy tufts of the marram grass and rye grass top the low dune and hold it more firmly. Back of this scant protection, low cottonwoods, willows, and sand cherries grow. The ridge shelters the area to the rear just enough so that the arbor vitae, tamaracks, and black spruces begin to build a defensive wall where enough of the requisite acid wetness is found in the hollow behind the little sand ridge to foster their growth.

The outer process of stabilization is virtually the same on any beach—the shore is one of the basic combat areas of the world. Sea beach or river beach or lake beach, shores of the Gulf of Mexico and Cape Hatteras and Cape Cod, of Florida and California, and of Oregon and Maine—sometimes the battle between loose sand and the rooting plants seems unending and never to be resolved. There

Beach pea

is always the restless conflict between open sand and water and the first well-rooted plants. Yet the formula for plant succession is condensed into one main fact: the sand *must* be held by pioneer plants before other vegetation may grow, before soil can develop and other forms of plant and animal life may live successfully. The sand pioneers serve their purpose in the world by beginning to hold the sand. This is so effective that wherever the protective cover inland is broken nature patches it up at once, not with the kind of material growing presently upon it, but usually going back again to beach rushes, wormwood, and the tenacious, trailing plants of the cinquefoil. I found that a break made in the plant cover in a three-foot-square area where a telephone pole's guy-wire had been recently planted near the road had caused this back-to-the-beginning replanting.

Plants of the shore are few. Although beach botany thus is a limited subject, it encompasses some magnificently sturdy and well adapted plants. The beach pea with its pale green-gray leaves and weak stems lies across the slope of the first dune and sand hummocks, and puts forth its large, purple-pink, sweet-pea flowers followed by slim green pods of peas. When the pods are ripe, they are eaten by the mice and song sparrows. The roots of these fragile-appearing plants go deeply and anchor themselves well in the loose sand; the leaves are coated with protective wax and are unharmed by the excessive heat of the beach.

The silvery cinquefoil is like a living piece of tough red-and-green cord putting down roots at intervals of a few inches and, in effect,

Cinquefoil

nailing itself to the sand. The clusters of roots go straight down and out, and have a powerful grip which makes the long, trailing plant difficult to pull up whole. The stem may break and leave the rooted portions where they are. Because the cinquefoil is in the same family as the strawberry, its character is explained—each rooting node sends up a new plant as the strawberry runners do. The leaves are compound with three to five pairs of leaflets arranged along a two-to-four-inch stalk, are sharply toothed, dark green above and silvery white below. The five-petaled, bright yellow, little buttercup-like blossoms on short, thin stems grow at intervals along the prostrate stem. Sometimes after rain and wind, the flowers are almost covered by sand, but they poke out, up to their necks, unhurt.

The sea rockets, with their lavender, radish-like flowers, are deeply rooted and, though fragile enough in appearance, survive a punishment which the majority of plants could not endure. So does the wormwood with its very deep tap root and lateral fibrous roots gripping the depths with startling tenacity. The ferny, silvery, basal rosettes have great beauty, but the tall, rather weedy stalks of small greenish composite flowers show the wormwood's connection with the ragweeds.

In spring I am surrounded by the pattern of shadows made by the wormwood lace, the embroidery of the cinquefoil, and the stark, inked, fence-shadows of the rushes; I am also surrounded by the little thin plants of rock cress whose small white blossoms whip madly in the mind. They grow in the harsh sand and survive beautifully with the other pioneers. These plants are all impressive in their growing and blossoming in an impossible situation. Only their innate hardiness puts them here.

THE HUNTERS

Animal life on the storm beach is wild and hungry, limited and transient, usually coming here only for food. Killdeers run along the water's edge, dodging the small surf—handsome brown and white birds with russet tails and black collars, they pipe and squeak and teeter, pecking at insects brought in by the waves. Turnstones may stop over in migration, and sanderlings are often here—both are birds of the seashores. There may be sandpipers, and there are always the gulls and crows. Sometimes blackbirds forage along the line of the shore for cast-up food. One day at the edge of the water I saw birds which seemed different from any shore bird I could remember. Excited with the possibility of something new, I raised my binoculars, focused—and discovered half a dozen plump robins using the food resources of the generous waves!

The beach is a land of the hunters. A large beetle called the fiery searcher, bronzy with scarlet undersides, came skittering along close to the water's edge, running with nervous haste and hunting with jerky movements. It was looking for dead insects and other creatures decommissioned by the lake. It not only eats the carrion, but also lays its eggs upon it, thus providing food for the young when they hatch as larvae.

As I watched the beetle move toward the gentle lift of the old beach level, that first low dune, a female digger wasp dropped down to the sand. Its transparent brown wings quivered with that nervous energy which possesses all wasps, especially on a warm day; its curling antennae darted nervously, probing the air. Quickly, the wasp commenced to dig into the loose sand, in the manner of a dog burying a bone in the pansy bed, making the sand fly out behind her in a fine shower. She was down in the hole, the sand still showering, then was out and gone before I realized she had quite finished.

Something else had been watching. A quiet insect, the fuzzy black and brown bee fly with its narrow gray-and-white wings and long trailing legs, had been dallying about in the air, hovering like a sparrow hawk, while the wasp was working. As soon as she was out of the hole and away, the bee fly dropped down to the hole's entrance, laid an egg just inside the opening, and was gone again, still not hurrying, still without any air of surreptitious meddling. The wasp did not return.

I was about to leave—the wind was strong, and further places called—when the wasp suddenly was back. She was coming slowly, flying low, lugging a paralyzed sand-colored spider which was almost as large as she. The wasp dropped to the sand near the hole, laid her prey down for a moment, coursed about nervously, as if nearsightedly looking for the entrance to the burrow. Then, her

Digger wasp

body pulsing, she came back for the spider and pulled the inert lump down into the hole.

In so doing, according to some instinctive calculation of the bee fly, she also very likely tugged in the egg, which was the reason why the fly had laid it there in the first place. Down in the hole, the fly larva would one day feed upon the paralyzed spider which had been originally provided as fresh meat for the young wasp. Because the bee fly cannot catch live food, its larva is thus parasitic on the wasp's industry and ability as a hunter.

Her own egg laid on the spider, the wasp emerged in a hurry, backed out, then made the sand fly in all directions as she closed the hole. She tramped anxiously about all over it, as if stamping it down to conceal every evidence that her egg was there. She was off, then, and doubtless never gave another thought to her young, to the spider, or to any chance of there having been a bee fly's egg. For that matter, the digger wasps very likely have no realization of the part which they unwittingly play in perpetuating the race of bee flies.

When the sand cools at night, some of its other populations emerge to feed. Mice and shrews forage across the sand, the one for seeds around the rushes and beach peas, the other for living flesh —often the mice themselves, or the hunting beetles, or the sand-colored spiders which live in little tunnels beneath the rushes and marram grass.

The shrew is a ferocious and deadly little animal. If it were larger —it is less than the size of a mouse—it would perhaps be one of the most feared animals in the world. It has a narrow, tapering snout; close, dark, sooty-velvet fur; and needle teeth. A poison gland in its mouth sends venom into its victim when it bites, and its prey dies quickly. One shrew has enough poison to kill two hundred mice in its brief lifetime. When this miniature killer comes racing in nervous speed and deadly intentness over the sand, the mouse is lost if it lingers. The beetle, the spider, the song sparrow's young—all will with difficulty escape.

Over the sand in the morning I find the fine, feathery tracktraceries of the small creatures which lived and died—tracks of mouse and shrew and beetle and spider and bird, records of the night's dramas on the dark beach. Other tracks are briefly held in the loose sand—the marks of killdeer, crow, and gull, lightly held and gone by the end of the day after the wind has broomed the beach. When the wind blows the long arching leaves of the beach grass in their incessant curves, those which touch the sand draw beautiful arcs as accurately as if with a compass, with some of the delicate footprint-traceries of mammal, insect, and bird, of hunter and of hunted, framed within them.

CHAPTER THREE

THE RIDGES

LIKE a wave embodied in sand, the low dune, with here and there the small white froth of sand cherry blossoming upon it, marked the end of the storm beach. Topped with the heavy grass tufts and low dune willows, the sand was halted—not really stopped, but at least it was pausing. It cannot be said to have been really held down until every part of it is covered, and this has not yet happened here. Nevertheless, from this point inland I turned a page in a living book of ecology.

In many parts of the once-glaciated areas of America, the records of the earliest periods of plant succession following the retreat of the ice were lost in the ultimate climaxes which occurred and in the alteration of the land by agriculture and cities. In this place the changes have been very slow, and the short summers and long winters have affected and slowed them. It is almost as if time had stood still, for in this place along the southeast slant of the Door Peninsula of Wisconsin, the pattern of what happened after the last period of glaciation has been retained in most—if not all—of its known phases from the open sterile sand to the climax forest. The spot is unique in the way in which it has kept intact the aspects of a cold-climate ecology in the midst of a warmer latitude.

Only a few miles away on the other parts of the peninsula, vegetation, in spite of the normally cold Wisconsin winters, is more southern in character. There, instead of coniferous forests and acid bogs, with their plants belonging in the Boreal Zone, the forest association is largely hardwood. Instead of the cold, acid bogs of the subarctic, there are meadows and streams which are decorated with glorious masses of marsh marigolds in May and a carpeting of green grasses all summer. There may often be a difference in temperature of more than twenty degrees F. between the lake and bay sides of the peninsula, only eight miles apart.

In a sort of living museum of plant life, the Ridges area near Bailey's Harbor retains the much more northern aspect of the boreal forest and its cold bogs and cedar swamps. Southward, this is largely extinct. Hundreds of miles northward it is still common. Isolated, remarkable, within a thousand acres there is told the story of plant changes and successions from the Ice Age to the present.

Through a fortunate chance, this place has been preserved, even though all around it the land has been logged, drained, or cleared for building sites. A long time ago in the age of sailing ships, the federal government established a range light reserve of forty acres at this place on the bay at Bailey's Harbor. Private owners held the surrounding acres. Some had cut off their timber, but others, perhaps fascinated by the peculiar wilderness of their property, or else discouraged from ever attempting to convert it into farm land, had done nothing with their holdings. It used to be the custom of the villagers to come with their children on Sunday afternoons in spring to walk through the Big Swamp, keeping to the dry ridge tops, to look at the wild flowers.

The lighthouse near the shore and the range light to the rear, by which ships lined up their positions in order to enter the harbor safely and not pile up on a reef, finally were no longer needed. In 1936 the government gave the land to Door County to be used as a park and campground. It was planned to cut it off, to drain and clear and turn it into a proper campsite for tents and trailers.

Even as the bulldozers were setting to work, public demonstration stopped them. Some of the determined women of Bailey's Harbor, having known and loved the place since childhood and realizing its scientific value, came out and stood defiantly in front of the machines until the men operating them had to stop. These objectionable females were then ordered to get out of the way, to leave off interfering with what was none of their business, and to go back to their kitchens where they belonged. The women refused. They simply held their ground, stood in the way, and halted the work for that day.

It was long enough. During that crucial time, others had been busy with the authorities of the Park Commission. Pressure, persuasion, and a wall of women got results. The Range Light Forty was to be set aside as a wild flower sanctuary.

But those who had won this first battle knew that they could not stop with this meager victory. There was a great deal more land in the Big Swamp adjoining the Range Light Forty, land which was just as valuable botanically and ecologically, just as full of boreal flowers as the original forty-acre gift. Land had to be bought and added before it was too late. To alter portions of the whole area would irrevocably alter and might ruin the rest, for the whole thing was dependent upon a delicate balance of acidity, wetness, and lack of drainage. Cutting and draining sections half a mile away could eventually tend to ruin the remainder. One swath cut in the wrong place, one draining of a slough, would begin to make any further protection too late. The whole wonderful and incredible area depended upon its balance of water and ridge and post-glacial vegetation for what it was and what it might continue to be.

People vitally interested in the project met in 1937 to form a corporation under the name of "The Ridges Sanctuary," and the

Garden Clubs of America donated a thousand dollars for purchase of more land. The purpose of the association was to secure—by purchase, gift, or by any other legal means—as much of the area as could be obtained in time.

Since then, more than nine hundred acres have been acquired. As recently as 1962, a ten-acre tract had to be hurriedly obtained with money borrowed from Nature Conservancy, to prevent its being taken up and cleared for a commercial site. Too late to be saved, land across the road had already been cleared and graded for a motel. Still more acres remain to be bought before the whole treasure is really safe. Dues of the association, benefits, and gifts all go for this purpose and for upkeep of the Ridges. It has become a place of pilgrimage for botanists from far places. Visitors who just like wild flowers number thousands in a season. Many can appreciate the outward beauty of the blossoms, but not all know their rarity and strangeness, their uniqueness, or their background, or much of the story of why these species are here.

I never fail to be impressed when I come to this aboriginal place. To get its full impact, I must go first to the edge of the water, as I have done today—face out to the south to the restless lake and the tumbling waves galloping into the bay, to the open sky, to the wind, and the flying birds—to feel the true genesis of this shore. Then I turn and trace my way through the successions of change, ridge by ridge, swale by swale, ending my peregrinations through time in a deep, old, virgin forest which adjoins the Ridges proper, yet is essentially part of it and its story. Perhaps one day the forest will be added to the protected acreage.

Since the area is naturally arranged in a series of long, half-moon humps and hollows, in general paralleling each other and curving as the ancient contours of the lake beaches did, each hump must mark the site of an old beach. Each one, successively remote from the present lake, possesses an older plant growth, a deeper soil, and a greater amount of shade.

The low places between the ridges are wet, but they are all

different. In some, fresh water lies in swales filled with sedges, giant reeds, and marsh grasses, where muskrats forage and where there are sometimes ducks and herons. In late May and early June some of the sedge swales are a flower garden of the spikes of white buckbean blossoms standing in the foot-deep water. In other hollows, the water is intensely acid and harbors bog plants such as the sundews and pitcher plants and the bog rosemary. In still others, the older ones, the shade is so great that it becomes a dark cedar or spruce swamp with thick mosses; brown water; small, rare orchids; and occasional splashes of marsh marigolds in spring. There is an alder swamp, and an ash swamp, each very different from the other and from the coniferous swamps and fresh-water swales.

To bisect this place, walking the crests of the low ridges and crossing on the small footbridges provided by the Ridges Association, is like taking a telescoped exploration over almost a thousand miles of landscape. It is as if, in going from the open beach to the climax forest, I have seen plants growing from Indiana to northern Canada.

The ecology student finds in these living things the examples of what he has read in perhaps tedious pages of required text. The philosopher finds proof of his assurance of continuity. The naturalist grasps within a small space the story of life in a land which the glaciers carved and whose influence is felt today.

Part of the strange effect of this place lies in the character of the plants themselves. Those which dwell here are, in many ways, the deprived ones. They have made the most of meager allotments of food, water, warmth, and light, and they have managed not only to survive but to thrive gloriously.

These boreal plants are the strange ones. They are the carnivorous ones, the saprophytes, the parasites, the plants which depend for life upon the presence of soil fungi, on cold, and on acids that would destroy many other kinds of plant life.

Exploring here, I found twelve situations emphasizing either too much or too little, and began to see not only how life managed to exist during and since the last glacier but how it can actually thrive on what appears to be extreme hardship, to make a place which is filled with an often austere but unforgettable splendor.

The haves and the have-nots—they are the ones which manage to live with too little water or with too much water, in too much sun or in too much shade, in too much acidity or with too little nitrogen, in too much heat and too much cold, in too long a winter and too short a growing period, in too much wind or in too little air. These are all situations to be abhorred by many plants. Yet in this situation of starvation and physical punishment which might destroy those which are native to lusher regions, I found a different assortment of plants for each association of life growing in each kind of habitat and on each different ridge and swale. In this closed community in which only the elect might live, the effete and the outlanders were excluded.

It is a place which is so uninviting to the introduced weeds and southern vegetation that few of them come in. If any do, they seldom survive for very long. An exception is perhaps a certain audacious dandelion which is growing on Wintergreen Ridge, dwelling ingratiatingly in the company of plants native to the Hudson Bay country and the subarctic, an intruder which is come upon with the shock of finding an anachronism of nature. It obviously does not belong here. The wonder is that it has stayed as long as it has.

The plants in this closed community have thus adapted to the three essentials they need for life—food, light, and water. It is the same stringent limitation which followed the great glaciation and is concentrated here with these vivid illustrations of the have-nots. They serve to populate it with some of the most interesting plants— more than two hundred species, thirty of them orchids—to be found in the northern hemisphere.

Uncompromising, yet as adaptable as the wasp, the spider, and the bee fly, the plants in the wild land lying behind the first ridge are all well suited to the environment of trial in which they live. Left over from an era long past, time pauses here to hold antiquity in the palm of its hand.

In a very short time, all these plants could be destroyed, the area quickly changed. Nature would, of course, begin an immediate repopulating, just as it did when the ice went away at last. Surely the bulldozing action of the glaciers was immeasurably more devastating than anything that man may devise. But we do not have thousand of years in which to stand by and watch the slow replanting, as the sand, left unguarded by pavement or lawn, would no doubt take on again the pioneer vegetation of the open beach. But the plants which would follow year after year in a changed and drained sand would not be those which are here today, these relics of the Ice Age. They would be plants which are native to the rest of the peninsula and areas farther south, with a preponderance of introduced weeds. There would no doubt be a long sequence of plant successions, in nature's methodical manner, but they doubtless would not be the same ones which are here today.

As easily as this, natural areas may be ruined or changed. It is for us, in no matter what part of the country, to guard the wild places, to hold on to them as something eminently precious and never to be truly regained, once they are lost. National parks, state parks, small back-country preserves, the clean brook through the meadow, the big woods in the river bottoms, the ancient plants of old dunes along the lakes—they are all part of America's background and possessions, part of our personal heritage. Our land is surely broad enough and has enough elbowroom in which to expand cities, build steel mills, and lay out superhighways, so that we may at the same time still hold to and cherish the wild places, the invigorating atmosphere of swamp and forest and lake and bog.

More than a hundred years ago, Henry Thoreau was an outspoken public conscience on the matter of keeping the wild places safe. For some of his radical views he was not especially popular with the more practical-minded citizenry, but this never affected his opinions or his utterances. He said:

THE RIDGES

"Our village life would stagnate if it were not for the unexplored forests and meadows which surround it. We need the tonic of wilderness—to wade sometimes in marshes where the bittern and meadow-hen lurk, and hear the booming of the snipe; to smell the whispering sedge where only some wilder and more solitary fowl builds her nest, and the mink crawls with its belly close to the ground. At the same time that we are earnest to explore and learn all things, we require that all things be mysterious and unexplorable, that land and sea be infinitely wild, unsurveyed and unfathomed by us because unfathomable. We can never have enough of nature. We must be refreshed by the sight of inexhaustible vigor, vast and titanic features, the sea-coast with its wrecks, the wilderness with its living and decaying trees, the thunder-cloud, and the rain which lasts three weeks and produces freshets. We need to witness our own limits transgressed, and some life pasturing freely where we never wander."

And he added firmly:

"From the forest and wilderness come the tonics . . . which brace mankind. . . . I believe in the forest, and in the night in which the corn grows."

THE WINDBREAK

A wind-punished, sun-blazed fence of trees rises beyond the first ridge with its low sand willows, its few young cottonwoods, and the balm-of-gileads with their fragrant, resiny buds and unfolding, sticky, dark red leaves. Arbor vitae, tamaracks, and swamp spruces stand up in a low row in the scanty shelter afforded by the low dune. Yet because of the protection of the dune which prevents water from draining away, they have enough moisture. The space

Arbor vitae

is wide between this ridge and the next, and is perhaps the widest of any space between any of the ridges. It is about three hundred yards from the first crest and the edge of the trees to the road and the big spruces on the second ridge.

In the 1870's, the shoreline was where the road is now. The sand and the plants between the road and shore today were all laid down and planted since that time. The lake evidently has receded rapidly in less than a century, yet it often rises again in periodic fluctuations. In less than a century, the sand has been nailed down and covered with a splendid carpeting of orchids, gentians, lilies, and some of that enduring ground cover which was perfected for use on the tundra—low grasses, sedges, horsetails, and small plants with creeping stems and roots. In some of the drier places in this particular problem spot where the sand has a tendency to break from its pinning and begin to move, the addition of long, trailing ropes of prostrate juniper, laced back and forth over the sand, serves to hold it in place.

Plant species which also grow on the tundra, or are closely kin to those that do, are characteristic of the ground cover behind the first wall of trees. Here are Indian paintbrush, fairy primrose, gentians, parnassias, arctic horsetails, and minute sedges two inches tall. Where natural ditches bisect the area and hold more water, the arbor vitae and spruces have grown well with their roots in water and cold sandy peat. In June I find the glorious blossoms of showy lady's-slippers, and in August the three-foot spikes of purple-fringed orchis. Calopogon orchids are bright pink butterflies in the full sunshine of summer. There are orange wood lilies and pink pyrolas, the ornamental spires of white camas and the tall wild irises, shrubby St. John's wort and bush cinquefoil. They were all given a chance to grow, given moisture, a bit of soil, and some protection from the wind, by that first sturdy windbreak.

The spruces, tamaracks, and arbor vitae or white cedars can withstand the persistent assault of wind, weather, and storm. They stand against a glaring sunshine whose heat and additional light are the greater for being thrown back from the open sand close by and from the snow and ice in winter. As many a gardener knows, the glare of winter sunlight reflected from snow upon evergreens may burn and destroy the tissue in the needles, more than the actual cold itself. These conifers at the rim of the ground cover have had to endure in and to thrive on too much light, heat, wind, and cold.

The arbor vitae have adapted well. If they had not been able to do so, they would have perished long since. In a shaded and more agreeable situation, their boughs are multitwigged, covered with bright, dark-green, oval scales laid in a braided pattern on branches which are spread in feathery, horizontal fans. But here in this exposed situation the twigs, as if in self-defense, have turned at right angles to the sun so that they are all presented edge-on rather than surface-on. They are arranged like the slats in a Venetian blind, and for the same purpose—to filter the sunlight, to let it in only partially and in useful, not harmful, amounts. The needles of these trees are yellow-green rather than the rich blue-green of those growing in the shade, and they are fewer on the twig. The difference between light and shade is visible even on the north sides of the low trees, where the twigs are in a little shade of the tree's own making. Even there they have begun to assume a more normal stance, spreading in the supplicating gesture of woodland trees instead of holding bony fists to ward off the blows of excessive light.

The tamaracks, with nearly enough acid water around their roots during most of the year, nevertheless seem stunted. Yet they have little problem with too much sun and wind. Their slender, short, soft needles are held in rosettes and tufts so that few take the full brunt of light or wind. In autumn the needles turn bronzy gold for a while and then fall off, and thus there is no problem with winter glare or ice.

The swamp spruces can take any hardship. They were the first trees to follow northward on the skirts of the glaciers, and they no doubt go farthest into the Arctic today. They hold their short, tight, dark-green needles in spiral rows, closely set around the twig and overlapping up to the bristly tip. The needles are protected with waxes, oils, and sugars to make them invincible. Thus they are kept from freezing in winter or burning in summer. I would guess that the swamp or black spruce of the north would perish if it had too much luxury, too easy a life with too much food or kindness or pleasant temperatures the year around. It is a tree which is built to fight back, and everything about its ragged form and its gnarly, tough, rough, sinewy twigs and trunk seems arrayed to defy defeat, disaster, and death.

As swamp-inured trees, these three in the windbreak can stand rooted in perpetually cold water for long periods of time, yet they can also take it dry. They seem to prefer the cold, acid peat, or the sand and peat which they find here. Armor-plated with their own particular kinds of protection, each tree has solved the problem of a difficult habitat. I found them later in other places, in much larger stands—in the great spruce swamp, in the tamarack bog, in the cedar swamp—but their representatives placed here were as guardians for the first small tundra-like plants filling the space from the trees to the road and the old lighthouse. Smaller trees were already scattered in this space, presaging the constant change which, many years hence, might put a coniferous forest in this now-open area.

GENTIANS, PRIMROSES, AND PARNASSIAS

As there was chara in the lake, so there must have been chara in the yesterdays of this landscape, for where it grew and deposited its marl we find certain specific plants. Grass-of-Parnassus and fringed

Fringed Gentian

gentians are two which are to be found in a chara-built underpinning distributed in the damp sand and earth. I had not suspected it up here in the sandy places, but, finding chara on the shore and discovering the parnassias and gentians, I dug down only a little way through the carpeting of plants to find a whitish deposit mingled with the sand—marl, product of that large alga, chara, serving to alkalinize the acid sands.

In August the parnassias will bloom with hundreds of creamy white bog stars poised on long slender stems above the small, low, spade-shaped, compact, gray-green leaves. Five petals are cupped around the stamens and the upheld pistil, and are marked as with the fine tracings of a crow-quill pen dipped in sepia ink. I always find great difficulty in photographing parnassias. They are not only continually whipping about in the wind as if they were alive, but the cupped flower stands so tall above the small, basal leaves that a close-up seldom gets all it should, while a more distant shot fails to show the exquisite markings of the flower.

The fringed gentians come a little later. Their tall, deep purple-blue cups are composed of four long petals which are held upright and somehow serve at first to enwrap each other. Their tips are fringed deeply in the unmistakable gentian character of elegance. They blossom through September, although I have found aftermaths even in October when the north was almost ready to put a final period to all its blossoms for the year.

On this spring day I found neither parnassias nor gentians in bloom, though the basal leaves of the former, like small, gray-green shovels, stood up on their short handles and were quite everywhere,

Grass of Parnassus

presaging their blossom-abundance later on. The blue of harebells dancing in the wind took the place of gentians, and in a bright and wind-shaken array I found hosts of small pink and white fairy primroses. Because of what lies behind its specific name, I like to call it the Mistassini primrose. Its botanical name is *Primula mistassinica*, honoring that northern Canadian river, the Mistassini, and that chill tundra lake and a tribe of Indians also bearing that name.

Fragile and thready, yet almost as tough as the beach grass, the little primroses, only two to six inches tall, withstand storms beating the traprocks of Lake Superior where they also grow, endure the chill climate and spring snows of the subarctic, and dwell in beds of thousands along the stony shores of Lake Michigan, or as here, in

Fairy primrose

the sandy ground cover. They are abundant all the way inland to the place where the big white spruces make just a little too much shade and kindness for their rugged constitutions. At some signal from nature, the primroses remain outside the area of deadly shadows. Delicate though they may appear to be, they thrive on wind and sun and on a punishment which could destroy many a larger plant.

The primrose sends up one or two wiry stems from a tiny rosette of almost invisible leaves lying close upon the ground or on the sand, or in a crevice in the rocks. There are three to six little lavender-pink, or rarely white, flowers, each with five notched petals and a flower tube rimmed with white and yellow. In some, the pistil reaches the top of the tube; in others it is short, and the stamens are visible in the opening.

THE RIDGES

Among the multitudes of dancing primroses, I found some of the tiniest equisetums or horsetails which I had ever seen. The northern carpet, in its necessity to create small, compact plants, has turned out truly minute equisetums—those descendants of coal-forest trees which once were a hundred feet tall. Accustomed to the more robust forms of these plants—some of the largest of which today may reach the noble stature of five feet, with fruiting cones at least an inch long—I was astounded to have to get down on my knees in order to examine these minute horsetails of tundra-persuasion, whose little cones were only about a quarter of an inch long. I needed a hand lens in order to marvel at their diminutive majesty. Their sterile

Arctic Equisetum

stalks with thready branchings were difficult to distinguish among the low matting of grasses and sedges.

THE CANADIAN CARPET

The matting may appear small, but it is certainly not insignificant. It exerts a power which is one of the great colonizing and planting influences of the north. The Canadian carpet is one of the most effective and at the same time one of the most ornamental ground covers to be found anywhere. Product of the Ice Age, it specializes in long, tough, extensive underground stems and widely spreading roots which at short intervals send up more low new plants. An attempt to dislodge one of the carpet plants is often virtually impossible; the effort only results in the ruin of the one finally broken off. The above-ground portion breaks, and the roots and underground stems remain in place to continue their long existence as if no interruption had come to the one small portion of it. The majority of the Canadian carpet plants feature thick, waxen, dark-green leaves which remain fresh under snow, but turn bronzy brown or reddish when exposed to winter cold and the reflection of sun on snow during the long glittering winter. Since most of these are only a few inches high, they are usually well protected under the insulating snow-blanket. This blanket is, in fact, one of the requisites for the existence of the Canadian carpet, not only sheltering it but also providing a vital and slowly released supply of moisture.

The name *Canadian carpet* serves to explain this cool, fragrant, northwoods upholstery which covers the ground and old stumps and logs with a delicious, compact, often wintergreen-flavored growth of evergreen leaves on low plants and vines. The plants never become large and leggy, are never weedy, never rank. I had been accustomed all my life to the overgrowth of plants in Illinois, Indiana, and Missouri, where most of the low-growing things in the woods vanish by mid-May and the woods are immediately taken over by tall, rank-smelling, often rather unpleasant plants like nettles and horseweeds and figworts, or by lettuces ten feet tall. In contrast, the sweet, low-growing, compact plants of the north are a perpetual pleasure, a cool ground cover characteristic of the Canadian Zone, that southern half of the Boreal Zone, dipping from Canada in only a few places into the United States. Canadian carpet plants, in the opinion of those who know and love them, constitute boreal botany at its best.

Although I find a carpet in the open parts of the early portions of the Ridges, it is more typical of cold, damp, moist old pine forests and mixed coniferous woods, of the cedar and spruce bogs, of beech-maple woods, and of arbor vitae and fir forests. In the Ridges, the place called Wintergreen Ridge itself, the second one back from the lighthouse, is occupied by a splendid array of carpeting richer than any Oriental rug, ornamented with orchids and colored sea-blue with dwarf irises, purple-rose with gaywings, scarlet and gold with paintbrush, and glorious deep green with compact, evergreen leaves. The basic color of the carpet is, of course, this dark green. The designs themselves are worked out in flowers which vary the pattern with every woods in which it is expressed.

In shade, the carpet plants reach their best and greatest variety and occupy much of the northern forest country. To come upon them in distant travels is like finding familiar and much loved friends in a suddenly clarified and understandable habitat. It was an assurance when we climbed the steep heights of Bonaventure Island out in the Gulf of St. Lawrence—the island where the gannets nest—and hiked the trail over the hump of the island to the rim where the great birds had their eggs and young. On the way we passed through familiar spruce-fir forest, carpeted with wintergreen and twinflower and mosses and ground pines. It was the same sort of carpeting we had found in woods above the Mohawk Trail in Massachusetts; in dark forests near Mount Chocorua and the Great Stone Face in New Hampshire; in spruce woods along Sheepscott Bay in Maine; in the forest at Newfound Gap in North Carolina's Great Smoky Mountains, where the Appalachian Trail comes through from Mount Katahdin, Maine, bound for Mount Oglethorpe, Georgia. And we came upon the pleasant familiarity of plants in the moose-haunted wilderness above the Bay of Fundy in New Brunswick, and in the Shick-Shocks and the Laurentians.

The carpet was growing on Mackinac Island between Lake Michigan and Lake Huron, in the forest around Lake Itasca at the source of the Mississippi, and on Isle Royale in Lake Superior, in forests lying in the great Quetico-Superior, shared by Ontario and Minnesota, and along the Gunflint Trail. It was also found in a dark spruce-fir forest on the way up to Fall River Pass in the Colorado Rockies. It was a logical thing to find, always in its proper place because it simply will not grow anywhere else, identifying

Bunchberry

that tremendous upholstering which was called forth by the post-glacial replanting following along in the chill, damp footsteps of the great ice.

The carpet often tends to form a mosaic of its closely-set plants. The mosaic may be composed of the shamrocks of the white oxalis, of rose moss and sphagnum whorls, or of the medallions of the bunchberry. The latter often forms great beds of itself, its whorls of leaves on short stems bearing in the center of each a miniature white dogwood flower. In August this is replaced with a fine boutonniere of scarlet fruits.

With the bunchberry may be the leathery, dark-green leaves of the wintergreen. The flowers and fruits come at the same time in August—pink-red berries flavored with essence of teaberry. The fruits remain under snow all winter, exist through spring and summer—those which are not eaten—and may still thus be found on the little low plants with their dark oval leaves when the white waxen bells of the blossoms start to bloom in late summer. To find wintergreen, and to eat a berry or nibble a leaf in the haunts of the northern woods, is to be properly initiated into a select gathering

Wintergreen

of those who know and understand these remote places and who find a personal satisfaction here.

Wintergreen, bunchberry—add to these the small trailing embroidery of vines of the partridgeberry with evergreen leaves often less than the size of a dime, a plant bearing bright scarlet fruits throughout the year and small, ornamental, pink-and-white tubular flowers decorated with white fur in July. The flowers lie close to the pine-needle carpet and possess a rich perfume which mingles with the aroma of the old needles. The partridgeberry fruit has what appear to be two blossom ends on one berry, and in fact it does—perhaps the only fruit so adorned. Two flowers trumpet out

Partridge-berry

of one ovary. In one, the pistil develops, and the stamens come to nothing. In the other flower, the pistil withers away, and the stamens mature and shed pollen. The combination produces a single scarlet fruit which is thus marked with two points of location of the blossoms.

A list of the carpet plants runs down a roster of some of the choicest vegetation of the north. Many are members of the heath family and are dependent upon certain small soil fungi on their roots in order to live in this exacting habitat. In this family are the cranberries, the blueberries, the bearberry, the wintergreen, and its miniature kin, the snowberry. For a long time, botanists felt that the snowberry should be in a family of its own, and so called it *Chiogenes*—snow plant. Only recently it was decided that although superficially the two are really not very much alike both the snowberry and the wintergreen belong in the family *Gaultheria*. Their most obvious point of kinship is their wintergreen flavor.

The snowberry tapestry is one of the most effective upholsterings of old rotting logs and tree roots in swamps. It is a petit-point creation of miniature leaves on tiny, intertwining vines. It lives not only in the damp, cool, coniferous woods but in deeply shaded, very damp, and highly acid cedar swamps. Here the wiry, trailing stems overlap and interweave and thickly conceal surfaces needing a year-round cover. The oval leaves, seldom more than a quarter of an inch long, end in a sharp point. The flower which comes in late May is about a sixteenth of an inch wide, a tiny, squarish, four-parted thing, exquisite under a glass. The hand lens which I carry in my hiking jacket is invaluable in finding the true beauty of a minute object like the snowberry's intricate blossom.

By August the flowers have matured astonishingly into small, oval, white fruits shaped like miniature watermelons one quarter of an inch long, delicately pulpy and flavored as with wintergreen and cream. The berries are half hidden in the matting of vines, but, sought out and carefully picked and eaten, they are among the choicest morsels of the north. The flavor of both the snowberry and the wintergreen is truly in itself a boreal flavor. It is found not only in these two, but very lightly in the partridgeberry, as well as strongly in the leaves and twigs of the black birch.

Growth in the snowberry is so slow—as it is in the majority of the carpet plants, which is of course the reason why they remain carpet plants and are not three feet tall—and so slight that a sixteenth of an inch is an acceptable annual lengthening of the

Snowberry

plant. A quarter of an inch in a year denotes an uncommonly favorable growing season.

Sometimes, especially very early in the season, the carpet is studded with beds of small plants which have scarcely any stem at all. One of these is the gaywings, *Polygala,* with a form and color which are both a good deal more orchid-like than those of many of the true orchids themselves. It is rose-purple, light pink, or occasionally white, with two flaring petals and a very elaborately fringed tube, each short white thread of the fringe tipped with pink and flaring to make a small sunburst.

With the gaywings, I often find the somewhat taller plants of American starflower, *Trientalis,* one of the primroses. It has an ir-

Starflower

regular whorl of shining green leaves making a free-form star, with the far more perfect white star of the flower itself poised on a slender stem rising from the center. There are plants with oval shining leaves, one or two to a plant, with a stalk of white froth between—the Canada mayflower. It is a lily, but the tiny flowers are stubbornly individualistic by having their parts in fours rather than in the customary threes or sixes which are acceptable and customary in the lilies.

In some woods are carpets of golden blossoms of the barren strawberry, *Waldsteinia*—I wish it had a better name—which is not a strawberry at all in spite of the name and the superficial resemblance to the plant. And accenting the low growth of the carpet are the larger plants with shining oval leaves, the clintonia. It has green-gold lily-bells in June and unique, ultramarine-blue, poisonous fruits, almost as large as cherries, two to six of them held upright on stiff stalks in August.

In the carpet there may be low blueberry bushes, coral-root orchids, pink moccasin flowers, ram's head lady's-slippers, and ferns. The carpet is intricately woven. It usually carries part of its pattern as an identifying mark, yet every woods has a somewhat different design, some variation, like true Oriental rugs, of which no two are ever created quite alike.

TRAILING ARBUTUS

The trailing arbutus is a part of the Canadian carpet. It is certainly one of the choicest plants of the north, perhaps known to more people than any other species found here. Long before any flowers are in bloom, when most plants are showing only winter-worn leaves or beginning to put out a new growth of leaves and flower buds, the arbutus has already come into bloom. The buds were made last summer, were showing petals last October, existed under snow all winter. By late April and May they open. Arbutus leaves are nearly two inches long, oblong, sometimes overlapping and hiding the flowers which lie in loose clusters on the pine needles themselves. But there are glimpses, and at the same time I get the full perfume of these blossoms, a scent which is compounded with the fresh odors of the damp sand and the old needles. It is a blending of the vanilla orchid's perfume with the smell of the northern spring. The combination is an unforgettable one.

The tubular flowers are held in small bouquets, are white and pinkish-tinged, sometimes all delicately pink, with five petals that

Trailing Arbutus

flare from the flower tube. The leaves are rather coarse and large in comparison with the miniatures of the snowberry, wintergreen or partridgeberry. They remain for several seasons, while new growth each year emerges, pinkish, fragile, and hairy, when the flowers bloom. The plant is prostrate and woody, sometimes a foot or two in length, making a trailing mat on moss and needles.

In arbutus time it is fitting to reread that poem, "Going Starring," by Robert P. Tristram Coffin, and feel anew the same delight as he when we turn back the leaves and—

> There is your star, a cool star made of snow
> That lay upon this hill and lately thawed—

I can never get enough of nature as it is expressed in the small perfections of the Canadian carpet. The very carpet is the signature of the place, as if in seeing it I did not need the presence of spruce or of fir, or the pines and hemlocks, or the lingering breath of the last glacier, to tell me what to expect here. The fulfillment is never dull, never outworn. It is exciting in any season of the year, because most of these plants are evergreen, and thus they are always neat and handsome.

Not all of the flowers blossom at the accepted time in spring. Perhaps it is because the carpet grows in land of such short summers and such long winters that there is very little true spring, as we know it southward. Summer is only a long spring, and autumn already is showing colors in mid-August when the wintergreen bells have just come into bloom. The partridgeberry, pyrola, and pipsissewa come in July, all charmingly sculptured flowers, from the low, white single star of the one-flowered pyrola to the intricate pink-and-white blossom-cluster of the elegant pipsissewa. But perhaps I come upon the greatest sustained display of flowers in June when the carpeting is full of the four-parted flowers of the bunchberry, and the shadowed slopes are decorated with hundreds upon hundreds of little pink-and-white bells of Linnaea, the twinflower.

JOURNEYS IN GREEN PLACES

TWINFLOWER

The twinflower was the favorite of the great botanist, Linnaeus. In his lifetime he personally found and named thousands of plants, from Lapland to Sweden and beyond, and received countless specimens sent to him by collectors around the world, at a time when scientific curiosity was sending numerous men to find out what kinds of plants and animals lived in remote places. But of all those which Linnaeus catalogued and to which he gave the names we largely use today, there was only one which was named for him, his favorite, the twinflower, Linnaea. He loved its small, close-creeping and rooting vines, the scalloped, sculptured, bright-green, tiny leaves, and the slender little two-or-three-inch stalks bearing pairs of delicate-pink, scented bells—a gentle fragrance which is best smelled as the arbutus is—down on one's knees.

In the world there is really only one species of twinflower, and it bears the name given to it by Linnaeus—*Linnaea borealis*. It is today still common in the coniferous woods and in the mixed woods of Sweden, as it was when the great teacher took his students on botanical excursions into the forest around Uppsala. It is really the very same kind which grows here in the Canadian carpet, for the flora of northern Europe and Asia is startlingly similar to the coniferous associations and the Canadian carpet in America.

Yet American botanists have tried to distinguish our species of twinflower by calling it *Linnaea borealis. var. longifolia*, a ponderous title which stretches out longer than many a twinflower stalk itself. The variation, if any, is insignificant. To the casual

Twinflower

THE RIDGES

observer there is really none at all, and what he sees growing over mossy slopes and old logs and around tree trunks and among the ferns, opening hundreds of pendant pink bells on a June day, is the very same twinflower which Linnaeus chose as his favorite. With this he had his portrait painted, the twinflower which in delicate design ornamented the best set of china used by the Linnaeus family on special occasions and now exhibited in the museum at Uppsala.

I do not mean to imply that the carpet is always an unbroken expanse all through the northern woods, because it is not. There are openings where pine needles cover the ground and little else grows but partridgeberry vines for dramatic accent, and ferns and moss clumps here and there, and now and again a clump of stark-white Indian pipe in late summer. But in many of the woods, where the carpet is present and unharmed, it is indeed pretty much all a beautiful upholstering, fitted with mosses in the interstices. There are mosses with golden, fernlike fronds, or clumps of white moss like rounded pincushions, or broom moss turned all in one direction as if swept that way. And there are the two-inch-high forests of *Polytrichum*, each plant tipped with a thready bristle bearing a little brownie cap, and the treelike plants of *Climacium*, the tree moss. The long strands of creeping ground pine and the other club mosses bind together the fabric. They unite the mosaics of bunchberry, the colonies of Linnaea, the wintergreen beds, and the studding of dark-green, three-parted leaves and white flowers of goldthread.

To explore the Canadian carpet country is full of small adventures. There is the chance of seeing a deer hock-deep in bunchberry; a porcupine, on its way to the next aspen tree, waddling through the ferns; the nest of a hermit thrush bedded beautifully in wintergreen at the base of a little spruce. And there is a chance of hearing the feathery concussions which are the drumming of a ruffed grouse—perhaps even of finding its nest somewhere in the contours of this magic carpet.

CHAPTER FOUR

THE PINE DUNES

As I walked up the sandy slope to where large white pines stood, their crests surging in the lake wind, I could still hear in the distance the steady roar of waves on the beach. The gulls blew over like snowy kites on the wind. The sand from which the pines grew was held in place with an interlacing of roots of the pine and spruce and juniper, and smaller plants. And because of the concerted success of the roots in growing, and because of the windbreak of trees, the sand now stayed well in place. The lower levels of dampness from the boggy swale below this ridge and the coolness of the short northern summer contrived to give much life to something which might have otherwise been arid and almost deserted. It was unlike the beach, yet it could never have begun to stay in place so successfully if the beach grass, cinquefoil, and rushes had not, perhaps many hundreds of years ago, first held it down. They were all gone from here now. The wall of trees between the ridge and the lake now held off the direct wind and its gouging action, and only the tree tops swayed wildly while the noise of the waves was a dim, incessant roar.

Knowing the restless character of the beach and first dune, it seemed strange to me to find such large and well grown trees in what appeared to be still almost pure sand. Yet they were putting down roots to moisture far below. They could obtain an abundant nourishment which they must have had in order to have become so well grown. Some of the white pines stood nearly seventy feet tall and had a trunk diameter of more than two feet. The white spruces were almost as tall. Their gray-green boughs spread broadly all the way down to lie on the sand itself where some of them, in great green fronds, appeared at times to have taken root. These low branches held the sand in place, too, and so did the prostrate junipers which spread their long, tough, ropy stems upon the surface of the sand, rooting at intervals. Their short, upright twigs were little more than six inches tall. Yet, if I should try to pick up one of these many-branched prostrate trees, I would see then how long it really is—that if the whole thing had the backbone to stand upright, it might be more than fifteen feet tall.

Like many of the alpine and tundra plants, the juniper chooses to lie close to the ground. The branches are studded with fruits which look like clusters of blueberries when ripe in their second year. At that point, however, the resemblance to blueberries ends. The juniper, like many of the elfin forest trees of the tundra, presents a certain obstacle course in a fast traversal of the pine dune—stated more succinctly, you can fall flat on your face if you try to hurry across this booby-trapped juniper patch!

This is a curious world of plants which are as highly specialized for their environment as are those of the bog, the carpet, or the beach. The pine dune, like the latter, is a world of hunters—chiefly the ants and ant lions; of parasites—the dwarf mistletoe and comandra; of strange fungi—the bird's-nest mushroom and earthstar; and of plants which have been joined, in ages long past, to make new entities—the lichens.

DWARF MISTLETOE

The dwarf mistletoe is little like the Christmas variety, is not even in the same family, though both are parasitic on trees. But whereas one simply borrows a little nourishment and a roosting place, the other does dreadful things to its host.

Dwarf Mistletoe

The common mistletoe was known and revered as sacred by the Druids and has been for many years a part of our holiday celebration at Christmas. The conspicuous, gray-green or yellow-green, spoon-shaped leaves grow in many-branching, brittle clusters, with twigs holding white berries which are sticky inside. It is found high in elms, apple trees, or oaks, in bottomlands in the southern states and as far north as Illinois and Indiana. The plant is propagated by birds, which eat the berries and then wipe their untidy beaks on twigs to remove the sticky material. Some of the seeds are left behind in a crevice to germinate. They send rootlike plugs into the bark and then into the wood, taking moisture and minerals from the tree's sap. This mistletoe, which is able to make food for itself in its green leaves and stems, seems to be relatively harmless to its hosts.

But the dwarf mistletoe in the spruce country does not make food, and it does harm the tree on which it must live in order to exist at all. It is a sinister little individual. The plant itself is so tiny that it is all but invisible; it is generally less than an inch high and is without any green coloring. The results of its presence on a tree are a good deal more prominent and easy to find than the plant itself.

When sunlight shines through the little stiff-branched plants perched among the needles of the spruce twig, they shine red or red-brown. The flowers are tiny. The little berries when ripe are literally exploded into the air and fly as much as sixty feet away—or so botanists say who have apparently found a means of checking the propulsion of a minute seed catapulted through the air and among the trees.

In order to sprout, the seed must fall upon and cling to the limb of a host tree, usually a spruce or a pine. Moisture causes germination. The tiny seed sends a small primary plug into the tree's bark, then probes deeply and peglike into the wood. In the growing tissue of the cambium layer, the mistletoe produces clusters of cells which become embedded in the wood to form cone-shaped bodies. These draw minerals and water from the living wood, the mistletoe's one source of life.

Its presence and insatiable hunger soon cause a strange and violent abnormality of the infected branches. From one tiny mistletoe clump there may spring a hundred or more distorted spruce twigs whose needles are stunted and often yellow-green and smaller than normal. Year after year the clump grows larger until the whole mass, seen from a distance, stands out as a great ball of dark twigs, often four or five feet in diameter. Sometimes the entire tip of a spruce becomes a witch's broom, grotesquely placed like a gigantic fur turban on the top of a church steeple. All below may be dead. Sometimes the brooms grow from lateral branches which eventually die. With the death of the tree the broom dies also, and so of course does the little ravenous mistletoe which caused the whole disaster. The curious thing, not yet thoroughly understood, is how this tiny, reddish-brown plant with innocently branching, coral-like arms, is able to cause a deadly distortion thousands of times larger than itself. This damage in spruce forests of the west amounts to a tremendous loss in usable trees, but in the extensive spruce forests and bogs in the north, the mistletoe may simply serve as a check on their too-great multiplication.

LICHENS

The pine-spruce dune was badly infected with mistletoe. Yet, since dead coniferous trees add a certain dramatic accent of stark black lines to the landscape, they were ornamental in their appearance rather than depressing. Some were swathed in the gray garb of long, tenuous Usnea lichens. Many trees, living or dead, had half a dozen different kinds of these strange, grayish plants, including the rosettes and medallions of many sorts of Parmelia and Cetraria upholstering trunks and boughs. Somehow, even the Latin names of the lichens have a stern and northern sound!

Reindeer lichens (LEFT)
Cladonia lichens (RIGHT)

Reindeer lichens, *Cladonia rangifera*, made a curly, gray groundcover in extensive beds beneath the pines and spruces, together with bright accents of the little rep-capped British soldier lichen, another Cladonia. In dry weather all lichens become very brittle; but after a rain or in one of the lake fogs which envelopes everything with droplets of life-giving mist, the lichens again become pliable. The reindeer lichens, on the day I visited this place, made soft beds of flexible growths resembling four-inch seaweeds.

The reindeer lichen is the favorite and often sole food of the caribou, deer, and other grazing animals of the north. To supply this necessary food for their herds during the tremendous winters of the far north, Laplanders gather lichen hay on the tundra late in summer and pack it away in bales which are doled out to the hungry domesticated reindeer all winter long. In the wild, these animals take long migrations each year to find new sources of the lichen. It is a very slow-growing plant; and if the deer remain to feed for too long in one area, they deplete the supply so much that the area is denuded and they may starve. In the vast reaches of the Barren Grounds in that northern wilderness, across the Arctic and the subarctic, there are miles of Cladonia, the reindeer "moss" or lichen, and because the reindeer themselves keep normally and perhaps instinctively on the move, the lichens are not obliterated.

Just as the reindeer is an animal of the bleak and hungry lands of the far north, able to subsist on a scanty diet in a harsh climate, so the lichens are able to survive in places where few other plants or creatures may live.

These strange, infinitely hardy, tremendously long-lived yet easily killed plants, the lichens, apparently came into existence very early in the evolution of life on dry land. There was little or no soil, and any plant which lived there must have been able to make its own place of rooting. Because of some need for combining forces against the threats to life on land, certain small white fungi, of no particular form or character, joined with certain insignificant green or blue-green algae. The union changed the outward structure, which was like nothing the world had seen up to that time, yet inside the lichen there still remained the distinguishable forms of both algae and the fungi, now living for mutual benefit in this new creation. Under a microscope, we may still find the parts of the two entities. More than thirty kinds of algae have been discovered in lichens; the species of algae, in fact, often determine whether the lichen can withstand open sunlight and heat, or if it must dwell in shaded coniferous woods.

Mingled with each other's structures, each aids the other. At the same time, they both have lost their outward identity as individuals in this co-operative existance in which tangled whitish masses of fungal thread or hyphae form the substance in which the algal cells grow. The fungus, which was unable to make food for itself when it lived alone, is enabled to obtain food made by the green coloring matter of the alga. The latter obtains not only a protective structure of great durability which prevents it from drying out too much, but also secures water from the fungus.

The pioneering lichens began to grow on the bare, archaic granites. At a time when there were no green plants but the algae, which had to stay in wet places, the strength and endurance of the made-to-order lichen, which needed very little water and only a dry, sun-beaten, wind-punished rock on which to grow, set about to conquer mountains.

These little low plants still wield a power strong enough to crumble granite and other rocks. The strong acids which are found in lichens are often the indicators by which botanists can determine the exact species of the plants themselves. These acids attacked the rocks—which perhaps had begun to crack and decay a very little through the onslaught of weather, with expansions and contractions caused by the heat and cold of day and night, and by water and ice—and crumbled them a trifle more. Generations of decaying lichen plants, mingling with the rock powder which formed as a result of the work of the acids, created a bit of gritty earth—or so it has been deducted from the very same action of the lichens today.

For hundreds of millions of years lichens have thus lived slowly and meagerly, have produced their teaspoonfuls of soil and have laid the groundwork of forests. Here in this place beneath the trees, on living and dead wood, on sand and on rock, they will perhaps, in some age thousands of years from now, have helped to build real soil.

They are at work everywhere on exposed granites and other rocks. Some lichens are so particular about their living conditions that certain kinds are to be found only on certain trees—the Parmelias often prefer the tannin in oak bark; Cetraria and Alectoria grow mostly on coniferous trees, chiefly spruces; others prefer acidic rocks, or calcium-bearing rocks, or damp sand, or cool, shaded earth in the deep woods. Some are so particular about their living conditions, requiring large amounts of nitrogen though very little else, that they grow only where bird excreta brings to the rocks this needed chemical. A brilliant orange lichen, *Xanthoria*, forms rosettes on shore rocks along the North Atlantic and upper parts of Lake Superior wherever the gulls have perched. It grows as well on the high peaks of mountains where eagles and ravens have their eyries.

Lichens are draped as tassels and beards from trees in damp northern forests. Species which hang on the Nova Scotia spruces in the land of the Acadians prove that Longfellow knew what he was saying when he wrote: "bearded with moss and in garments green . . ." They are especially abundant in the north where a heavy lichen growth is fostered because of the general coolness and humidity, the shortness of the summer, and the nearness to the lakes or ocean which regularly send fogs to add to the moisture in the air.

Yet lichens also thrive in places of heat, exposure, aridity, cold, and despite a lack of food. They grow in places where other plants usually find life intolerable. It seems that no degree of privation hinders lichens—they thrive on it. In fact, if a lichen has too much water and too much food—is too well treated—the plant may simply exhaust itself with overeating and die. Its metabolism is evidently geared only to the spartan existence.

When a lichen is dampened by rains, it absorbs water, then retains very little of it in the tissues as the remainder evaporates. Since lichens cannot give off poisons which may be taken in with the water, these plants soon die in cities where air pollution is a menace. The waning lichen populations or their complete absence are in fact one of the indicators of the seriousness of unseen poisons from motor car exhausts, factory smoke, gas, chemical sprays, and other airborne impurities.

Lichens need the clean air of the wild places; they are part of the landscape in some of the grimmest regions of the world where they seem always to have served as emergency rations. The dry black scales and rags of rock tripe, Umbilicaria, growing on rocks of the Barren Grounds in the Arctic, saved from starvation the hard-beset men of Sir John Franklin's Arctic expedition in 1819. Every lost hunter or explorer might stave off starvation in lichen country. Although rock tripe often can be a nauseous diet, it nevertheless has more than a third more calories than the same amount of honey or corn. This same species helped to sustain Washington's men at Valley Forge, though certainly none of them liked it. I find the flavor of the very similar lungwort lichen, Pulmonaria, in the northern woods, to be not at all disagreeable—but then, I am not compelled to rely upon it as a sole article of diet.

In spite of the lichen's strange power of maintaining life and giving nourishment, perhaps no one but the reindeer really has relished this plant as steady fare. Self-sufficient, undemanding of space needed by anything else—ancient, life-saving, soil-producing plants—these are the lichens. Among the spruces on the ridge, they were all about me that day.

EARTHSTARS

Lightly placed on the sand beneath the pines and scattered in gnomish constellations among the reindeer lichens and the prostrate junipers were some other curious creatures—the little earthstar mushrooms. They are one of the fanciful creations of the lowest orders of plants. Like the bird's-nest fungi, the scarlet cups, the black chalices, the elfin saddles, the miniature clavarias, and countless more of the small, little-noticed yet fascinating fungi of the

Earthstar

woods, the earthstar is one of the special surprises I like to come upon.

The earthstar is in the same great family as the puffball and, like all fungi, is propagated by means of spores instead of by seeds. In some mushrooms the spores are formed as a fine dust in the gills which are placed on end like fragile knife blades beneath the cap, or in pores, or in pits on the surface of the mushroom. In the earthstars and puffballs, the spores are formed inside the globular body of the mushroom itself, the peridium. This, in the earthstar, is double skinned. The outer skin of the miniature globe splits and peels back like the segments of a tangerine rind to make a star with from five to nine points. From a small opening in the tip of the inner peridium, the dried spores burst and fly away by millions—nine *trillion* spores may be released from one large fungus during its brief reproductive life.

In wet weather the earthstar usually opens its points so that they lie back and the whole mushroom is lifted off the wet sand, like a starfish humping itself. With the return of dryness, the arms usually fold around the peridium again, although after the spores have been pretty well dispersed the arms frequently remain outstretched or curled under in all weathers.

The earthstar is a durable creation. It normally forms in autumn; yet those which I found scattered in a vague sort of constellation on the sand on a May day had been left from last year, had had heavy snows piled on top of them, and then had lived through the thawing. They still puffed a few spores when I pressed a peridium. These earthstars were small, little more than an inch wide, some even less than that, but I have found other sorts which were four or five inches in diameter and were gray, pale brown, or a beautiful rosy-tan color.

BIRD'S-NESTS

A dead twig beneath a pine held an array of most astonishing miniatures stranger than the earthstars. Ranged along the twig were

Bird's Nest mushroom

tiny fungus nests, complete with minute "eggs." If I hadn't known what they were and how they came to be here, and if I had been a trifle superstitious, I could have thought them truly to be the eggs and nests of some incredible fairy bird. The nests were only half an inch in diameter and some were less than that, while the eggs, both in size and color, were very much like puffy sesame seeds.

With earthstars, nature seemed to have gone overboard in making something elaborate; the simple puffball shape would certainly have been just as effective. In the bird's-nest mushroom, nature in fact has become so downright whimsical that not even the tricks of hiding quartz crystals inside a geode or making the hawk moth to look like a hummingbird are much more surprising. In contriving for intricate reproduction methods in one of its lowliest forms of life, nature is impressive in the creation of the bird's-nest mushroom.

Yet, in nature there is no greater and no lesser importance placed upon one creature or thing over another. Each in itself is important because it *is* itself. If it is successful in being itself and in reproducing its kind, then, no matter how fanciful, or how small, or how ridiculous it may seem to us, it has a place in the world. If it is unsuccessful, then it becomes extinct. Nature may seem whimsical at times, but it is also terribly final.

The bird's-nest fungus is a half-inch cup attached to dead wood or other once-organic debris, usually in closely set colonies. Behind the back fence I once found an old board which was encrusted with more than a hundred of the tiny, pale-yellow nests. Those on the pine twig were somewhat larger than the yellow kind, and were arranged with considerable dignity and aplomb along the stick. Each brown cup, a straight cornucopia, stood erect and was ornamented with thin lines and ridges down the sides; each had a noble black fringe upright around its opening. Down in the bottom were the tiny "eggs." They ranged from six to a dozen and were fastened to the bottom and walls of the nest like eggs of some nearly microscopic bird.

These eggs, often a trifle smaller than sesame seeds, are the spore cases, the peridioles. They contain thousands of spores. To many botanists for a long time the puzzle was to discover just how the spores broke out of their hard shells, and how they escaped from the beautiful little nestlike cup. Each peridiole was firmly attached with a strong, fibrous cord to the wall of the nest. How then could it become detached so that the spores might be released? Or were they released from the eggs while they were in the cup? Some nests had no eggs—the deduction was that in some way they must have removed themselves from the container, but the method of removal was quite unknown.

But, as always in nature, reason governs arrangement. The cup happens, by design, to be just the size to receive a raindrop. During a rainstorm, one pelting drop hitting the cup makes a splash—and its force serves to knock out the spore cases. The cord which had fastened each one to the wall now extends lengthily in long, fine, silky threads. As the peridiole is suddenly thrown out of the cup, the threads follow in a tiny comet-tail. The egg may fly three to seven feet away. As it lands on a twig or leaf, the threads, in the momentum of the ejected body, wrap themselves, bola-fashion, around the nearest object.

As if this strange event were not wonderful enough, what comes next is even more astonishing. Nature, appearing to be rather careless at times, is probably the least careless force with which to contend. Since there is always a reason for everything, there is one for this small circumstance which, in a shower, has caused a raindrop to knock the eggs out of a bird's-nest mushroom and hang them on a bush.

Suspended thus among the leaves, the spores have now suddenly joined the available food for browsing animals—for deer or cow or horse. These spores, in order to grow, evidently must be eaten by an animal, must pass through the animal's digestive system and be voided, before they may germinate to produce more strange little bird's-nest mushrooms.

ANT LIONS

It was in this place of astonishing miniatures that I came upon the lairs of the lions in the sunny sand—ant lions, that is. Small, funnel-shaped pits dimpled the sand—inverted cones an inch or two in diameter across the top, tapering to the bottom perhaps

Ant Lion
ENLARGED ABOUT
10 TIMES

an inch deep in the sand. The pits seemed open, sun-parched, unoccupied, as if a troop of gnomes had been digging for treasure and then had gone off, leaving their diggings unattended.

Yet as I watched an ant came racing along in a tearing hurry as if late for an appointment; it was knocking at the boulder-like sand grains in its rush. The ant did what all of its kind seem obliged to do when the ground level changes or an obstruction looms. In that dogged, one-track purpose of the ant, there is no going around, never an easy way. It must climb up and over, or down and under and up, must laboriously scramble up the other side or down the other of any hindrance on its route.

THE PINE DUNES

The ant, therefore, did not bypass this pit, but started down its slope. Immediately the loose sand grains cascaded after it, bowled it over, and the ant, struggling and upset, quickly landed on the bottom of the little funnel. Before it could get itself assembled and start up the slope, a demon hidden in the bottom was kicking sand out from under the ant. Two pincers reached out in a lightning jab.

The ant struggled only briefly before a paralyzing secretion from the jaws of the demon—the ant lion—rendered it motionless. The victim was drawn down out of sight in the sand where I assumed the lion was feeding. Evidently having sucked the juices quickly from its prey, it suddenly flipped the empty carcass, like a discarded sandwich bag, out of the pit.

I dug out the ant lion. It disliked the sudden, unprotected glare of sun and scrutiny and seemed to cower, a pudgy gray, furry sort of creature with powerful pincers but no other outward distinction. It is the larva of *Myrmeleon,* a winged insect shaped something like a small damselfly or a very slender, delicate dragonfly, and is related to the lacewings. As a nocturnal insect, the adult is snapped up by night-flying birds, but the larva, hidden in its pit, is not so easily apprehended or destroyed by any enemies which might seek it. The only menace I can think of is the flicker which often comes down on one of the big ant-nests nearby, as if to his private picnic table, to dine on the residents. It would be simple enough for a flicker to apply his attention to the lion pits.

There certainly was plenty of food to sustain both ant lions and flickers. This pine zone where the sand was carpeted with juniper, bearberry, and reindeer lichens contained some of the largest ant-nests I had ever seen. For a long time I could not understand the size of these structures—great dome-shaped or flat-topped hummocks, often with small leaves laid upon them, and sieved with holes into and out of which innumerable large black ants were always running. A bushel basket might with difficulty be squeezed over the top of the colony located near the big pines, so large that it would seem that the weight of the sand itself would prevent any tunnels or chambers from being made or kept open by the occupants.

But inside was a loose arrangement of dried plant remains, including the long-lived, waterproof, and durable lichens, which held the sand apart so that the rooms and hallways and nurseries might be maintained. A colony of this size may remain for many years in the sand and in the slight shelter of the junipers, bearberries, and lichens. Yet one really hungry flicker could destroy it in a day or so.

DWARF LAKE IRISES

I came upon another large nest rising like a mountain among the dwarf lake irises, some of which were with difficulty pushing up through the slopes of the ant hill itself. The sands that day were almost hidden in some places by those widely spreading beds and

Dwarf lake iris

borders and masses of flowers which were the color of lake water on a bright day—the dwarf irises of the upper Great Lakes. Although the pine dune areas are to be found across the upper part of the United States, from Cape Cod to Minnesota, containing many of the same things I was finding here that day, it is perhaps only in these cold, sandy haunts of the lakes that the little irises are to be found. Rising from a weak, slender, yellow rhizome loosely set in the sand and held down by only a few roots, the irises send up short blue-green leaves less than four inches high and stalks which each produce two or three flowers. These open one at a time, day after day. They are flat blossoms two to three inches wide, of a brilliant amethyst-purple-blue which has that lovely sheen of the iris. On the three spreading, petal-like sepals is a broad, white-fringed blotch of gold.

The little iris is one of the unexpected charmers of the rare, glacier-affected places where it grows, blossoming in great numbers to form pools and rivulets of color. Knowing that many of the wild flowers of the midwest and north came from the Smoky Mountains area, I wonder the more about these infant-sized irises. On trails in the Smokies I have come upon another dwarf iris which is very much like this one, only somewhat larger. It grows in a far different sort of habitat, yet perhaps, at the end of the Ice Age, the irises which migrated northward, coming to rest here in the inhospitable sands of the newly-formed upper lakes, had perforce to become smaller because of the poor food and short growing period.

BEARBERRY

Nearby spread the dense mats of bearberry, one of the heaths, and a sturdy pioneer plant of tundra, rocks, mountains, and sand, one of the Canadian carpet plants. It is native to dunes and other harsh environments, bringing evergreenery and beauty and a covering for bare places wherever it grows. The bearberry roots are so interwoven in the colonies of creeping, foot-high plants that a single plant is long since eclipsed in the colonial aspect. The stems are tough, woody, resilient, and mightily enduring. They curve up from the base to lie out on the sand or rock, the tips uplifted, the leaves

Bearberry

oval or spatulate, dark, glossy, leathery, and very durable. They are protected from excessive sun, cold, and wind by waxy layers of cells overlying the green, and by a supply of oils and sugars which add protection in cold.

It is green the year around and for a large part of that time holds clusters of dark-red, tasteless berries which are sometimes called "chipmunk apples." However, I am most pleased to find the bearberry when it is in bloom. Clusters of little pink and white bells are held with a great elegance on each uplifted stem. In my opinion, the flower of bearberry, Arctostaphylos, is one of the most beautiful in the north, that realm of the small and the exquisite. Created in the classic Greek-vase form of many of the heaths, each set on a tiny star-shaped calyx and held in clusters, the little flowers are sparkling white. The almost-closed, five-scalloped lip of the bell appears as if dipped in pink paint.

I had always thought of them as little Greek vases, as the embodiment of perfection in the heath family which specializes in sculptured bell forms in many of its flowers. But, in exploring this region around the lake, I learned a new name, a homely one but one with much meaning. Miss Emma Toft, who has lived nearby since girlhood, had known the bearberry flowers long ago. She and her friends used to call them "lamp chimneys"—and these flowers surely are like little chimneys for old-fashioned oil lamps. Here in the dune, then, were hundreds of miniature pink and white chimneys—vases—bells. Although they were such a special part of spring in the north, they were also a part of the high mountains and other severe haunts around the upper part of the world.

And different from iris or bearberry, yet found on this ridge and on the next, lived the small and rare ram's-head lady's-slipper. This is one of the uncommon and most sought orchids in America and, true to the orchid tradition of elusiveness, has the quality of being invisible while at the same time it is in full view.

THE PINE DUNES

RAM'S-HEADS

Even though I knew that the ram's-heads grew there, and had indeed tracked them down the year before and so felt very sure that I knew exactly where to look for them—there among the little irises and gaywings, there along the edge of prickly juniper—I could not find them at first. They were rather like the sundews in the bog—invisible, until suddenly they were all about. Thus, in a spot which I had passed twice before, hunting carefully, and to which I then returned to examine over again, I found a fine clump of slender, eight-to-ten-inch stems topped with those curiously goatish profiles of the ram's-head lady's-slipper. They had, of course, been there all along.

Ram's Head Lady's Slipper

The flower is little more than an inch in length unless you include the flaring sepals which enlarge it top and bottom. The color is a purple-maroon with a bronzy tinge, and on the slipper portion white lines are drawn in a nice accent. Long, white, furry hairs further create that illusion of something beloved of Pan, the goat-footed god.

The lady's-slippers, gaywings, and irises grew in some shade, at least during part of the day, but the Indian paintbrush, white camas, and northern comandra all were mostly in full sunlight. That sunlight in summer must be twice as bright, twice as hot, twice as devastating as in some areas because it is thrown back from the open sand itself. Probably because of the lack of food in the sand, both the paintbrush and the comandra grow as parasites on the roots of other plants. The comandra evidently prefers those of pine, but the paintbrush must satisfy itself with lesser plants. I have often found it in open places, as well as high on the treeless alpine tundra. Flaring with tubular bracts of neon-scarlet accented with green and brass-yellow, the paintbrush plumes illuminated the day. Even on a lowering, dark-gray day in the fog, the paintbrush maintains that curious, deep-seated glow in its brilliant flower tufts.

It seemed to me that a good many of the plants in this deprived area (except for the pines and spruces themselves, and they, too, might be dependent upon soil fungi for their own support) were dependent upon something else for their very existence. The lichens needed support, humidity, and nitrogen which they could not sup-

Gaywings

ply for themselves; the orchids needed fungi on their roots to enable them to grow; so did the bearberry, the arbutus, the wintergreen, and the pyrolas in carpet-areas. The mistletoe needed the sap of pines and spruces; so, in a different way, did the comandra and paintbrush. The ant lions preyed on the juices of ants and other insects. The flicker was attacking the ant lion. And a digger wasp was furiously digging a pit to bury a spider she had caught and into whose own juice she had injected her paralyzing, preservative poison. Predatory, sucking, half starving—these were some of the inhabitants of the pine ridge.

But in the distance again I heard the sweet, broken chanting of a hermit thrush, a bird of the cool spruce bogs. A warbler exploded a hurried song in the nearby swale, beyond which I saw, standing in shallow open water, hosts of white hyacinth-like blossoms of the buckbean, Menyanthes, a plant of northern swales and bogs far up into the subarctic. Their flowers were white stars, thickly feathered with upstanding white hairs, accented by purple-black stamens and the gentle pink of the buds.

A chickadee foraged among the lichens on a pine trunk. The gulls still cruised overhead, blown on the wind yet always in command of the situation and tying together the changing units of landscape over which they flew and in which I walked. Far out beyond the trees I could still hear the distant roaring of waves on the punished beach. And I headed inland toward the song of the hermit thrush, to the Canadian carpet of Wintergreen Ridge, and the cool, fragrant, mossy bogs, spruce swamps, and deep forests which the bird's presence portended.

CHAPTER FIVE

THE BOG

THERE are splendidly boggy places in the Ridges, but they are situated only narrowly in the long, curving swales between some of the sand ridges themselves. To see a true and more comprehensive story I must go farther north to where there still lie thousands of glacier-created lakes whose rims are slowly filling in with bog plants, or have long since completely closed to become muskeg. When the Ice Age was ending and the glaciers were leaving pockets of buried ice or standing melt-water, the result was those innumerable lakes in Minnesota, Wisconsin, Michigan, Maine, New England, and much of Canada.

Each such body of water, although so similar in design, origin, and structure, has its own character. If you are familiar with such a lake, perhaps have vacationed beside it or known it otherwise, then your lake is a very special one and has deep meaning. I, too, have a special one which tells its story with vivid illustrations.

Beyond the trees, the lake lay in the pink light of a northern sunset. Smooth, mysterious, voiceless, reflecting the tall, inked spires of spruces along the rim, with a horizon of ragged spruce and leaning tamarack, it was the embodiment of all that a northern lake should be. I could feel its wonder, might sense some of the things which were part of it but which I could not see. In that reflected color, the water sent up a trifle of mist, blurring the rosiness just enough to give it an added mystery. I heard a loon but could not see it, could only listen to the wild and wonderful melancholy of its crying in the pink light and the mist.

The voice echoed against the pine hills to the west, which threw back the sound twofold as the bird then came hurtling into view, a dark projectile, yodeling. It went up and down the length of the lake twice over, flying and crying for the pleasure of it, and then as it came back I ducked instinctively as the bird suddenly slanted over my head and came down on the lake. It hit the pink water with a splash that sent lavender spray into the air, was down on the mirroring of the lake. For a moment, the whole unreal thing had seemed too breathless to believe. Then, watching the bird with its sharp, heavy beak held at that definitive loon angle, I saw a deer on the point of muskeg.

It had been standing so quietly that I suppose I had taken it for a stump or a low tree. It was picked out in silhouette in the fading pink light and mist. This was the kind of place and the time of day in which a moose could be expected to lift a dripping muzzle from among the water lilies; but just now the deer would do, and it was infinitely satisfying and wild. The whole scene—the broad, cool, mysteriously vaporous lake, the muskeg on its rim set with black trees, the deer, the loon, the gutturals of the green frogs, the distant fluting of the hermit thrush, the white-throated sparrows piping somewhere in the blueberry upland behind me—was what I shall always remember as embodying this north country and its waters.

Wolf Lake by day was scarcely less alluring, but it was many years before I came with companions and portable boats to find out what it was really like and to explore its farther reaches. Located in Nicolet National Forest, about ninety miles south of Lake Superior, the lake was not really very close to anything. Only at one small portion of it did a forest road touch briefly before going off again into the hemlock and pine forests. The rest of the lake was so completely surrounded by its miles of wilderness, most of it apparently boggy, that no house, summer cabin, or road existed except the one forest road just touching the south end. Few fishermen came here. The lake was left quietly to itself and to the occupancy of the wild.

It had always called to some of us to find out more of its secrets. But the years went by, and there were other things to do, other places to explore, mountains to be hiked, rivers to be comprehended. Then one summer morning we who were back in the north formed an expedition to go to Wolf Lake, to take a kayak and a john-boat along to explore the shores and find out what was beyond the bends and bays, to discover what might lie on that distant horizon of ragged spruce and tamarack.

The fact that the lake was almost totally surrounded by muskeg and quaking bog had not been apparent until we started out in the boats. The marvel was that there should have been any solid shore at all on which to build a road! This south portion, the highest part of its present shore, was composed of large gravel deposits left by the last glacier, which no doubt had dammed up this particular lowland during some of the final hours of the Ice Age to make a lake.

They were clear, cold waters which for some time must have been as lifeless as the country around them, but not for very long. Birds coming up from the south to the newly released, wet lands below the glacier must have brought on their feet the spawn of fish and clam and crayfish and snail, the spores of algae and the seeds of pondweed and milfoil. It is hard to comprehend the total repopulating of an area, but however it was accomplished, life indeed came. The waters were filled with it, and so were the once lifeless sandy, gravelly shores and glacier-heaped hills of gravel round about. The lake was large then, perhaps half a dozen times greater, or even more, than its length today, which must be a little less than a mile. As the generations of water plants died and built up sediment on the bottom, and as land plants growing on the wet edges, needing more room, leaned over and left their remains in the shallows and finally began to root there, the lake became less and less deep and clear, more full of living things. It also became a little smaller in its total dimensions because of the boggy rim which was building out its edges.

THE SPHAGNUM

Apparently this had its actual beginning when a certain small sedge, *Carex lasiocarpa*, started to grow on the wet shore, then floated on its widespread roots in a tangle of algae and other plants which buoyed each other up in the water itself. Soon the sedges had made a floating mat, the one supporting the other; the mat was made possible chiefly by the interweaving of the sedge itself. Sphagnum mosses came in, filling the mat with dense growth, but the sedges, small yet very persistent, were still crowded into the colonies of wet moss. The whole structure formed a thick, spongy rim almost all the way around the lake shore. It continued to extend

Sphagnum

slowly, through the centuries, into the open water.

It was the common sequence of bog formation. In some lakes this finally took place quite all the way around the lake so that the growing bog was like the cake part of a doughnut and the open water slowly growing less in the middle was the hole. At Wolf Lake the high ridge of gravel pushed up at the south end by the bulldozer action of the ice evidently did not foster bog growth and only here was the lake edge left open, occupied by a few water lilies and bullrushes growing up in clear water above sand.

This bank of gravel is what keeps Wolf Lake from running out and destroying itself, for the land drops off into a deep valley on the other side of this natural embankment. The valley itself, however, may have been made long ago by the great drainage out of the lake when it was considerably higher, until the dammed-up portion finally stopped the flow of water and the remainder of the lake stayed in its present area. If that bank had been washed out or scoured out by the ice, the lake would not have been created—a lake that sparkled in sunshine yet still held some of the mystery of that distant pink sunset and mist, of the black trees, the deer, and the flying loon.

I suppose none of us had realized how much of the lake was already filled with bog until we started out in the boats, or perhaps had grasped the immensity of power in the weak plants of the sphagnum moss. To see a bog which may have been growing with countless uninterrupted generations of this moss and its associated plants for perhaps eight thousand years or more is to see what that substance has accomplished and what it still intends to do.

In this cold lake water, vegetation does not decay and disperse its gases as it does in warmer waters. Therefore, a great piling up of undestroyed dead plant matter takes place, chiefly the myriads of generations of sphagnum which, by means of cold, time, and pressure eventually may form peat. Because of the cold and the lack of nourishment, root growth is very slow in the acid water. Plants must live lives of chill poverty and must supply their mineral and vitamin needs in other ways than by taking them up in their roots. Therefore, only plants which are especially suited to such conditions are to be found here. Many of them have dry, evergreen leaves—the leatherleaf or Cassandra, the cranberry, laurel, Andromeda, Labrador tea—whose structures are fitted for deprived conditions. They thrive in acid peat, in short summers, and in the long, terrible winters whose deep snows are what save them from the ravages of great cold and dessicating winds. Cool summers and snowy winters, in fact, are among the requirements of the northern bog plants, the salvation of all plants growing in the north, and the basic character of the land just below the glaciers.

The sphagnum moss is a wet and spongy plant—perhaps it is never a single plant, really, but a colonial growth of many. The individual plant is seldom or never found unattended, for sphagnum grows in great beds of thousands, all the long, weak, watery stems supporting each other in a beautifully upright position. Sphagnum is very large for a moss, perhaps largest of all. Each fragile stalk is topped with a rosette of long, soft, feathery, pale-green leaves, with similar leaves clothing the stem loosely down to a point well below the light. After that the stem is covered with the brown scales of old leaves which, far down, may form a thick, matted, wet brown muck. The upper leaves are pale because the green cells occupy only half the space in the plant—they are arranged alternately with colorless cells which may contain water or, in extremely dry weather, may be empty and white. Sphagnum has the power to hold much water, even to absorb it from the air.

The empty cells also add buoyancy, and they can store water for the times of drouth when everything else is dry. Yet, because of this spongy quality of the moss, the bog stays wet. When full of water, the sphagnum becomes so heavily saturated that a handful, squeezed out, often renders more than half a cupful of water. In late summer and autumn, much sphagnum turns a rich dark red.

So many of the nothern plants, especially those in bogs, turn red in late summer. This characteristic may be related in cause to the same combination which turns tree leaves red in autumn, for one of the chief factors in producing bright red leaves is a nitrogen deficiency. Others are cold nights and sunny days, all of which the bog plants certainly have. Whether or not there is also the chemical anthocyanin in these same bog plants, as in the leaves of maples and sumacs and many more, I must some day find out.

CASSANDRA AND ANDROMEDA

And so, through the centuries, for thousands of years, the bog had been very slowly expanding around the shores. In the bays it had now become solid, so solid that, for lack of expansion laterally,

Andromeda

the sphagnum has had to hump itself into rounded tussocks which the Indians called muskeg. On these hummocks grow the bog laurel, the Cassandra, and the Andromeda. All three are low, tough, twiggy bushes, and the latter two have lovely Greek names.

In Greek mythology, Cassandra, the daughter of Priam, was given by Apollo the gift of prophecy, but the gift was ruined when Apollo would let no one believe any of her warnings. Cassandra of the bog—pearl-flowered, bushlike—prophesies solidity beneath but grows always in an uneasy bog terrain.

Andromeda was Queen Cassiopeia's daughter who was chained to a rock to be eaten by a dragon but was rescued by Perseus. Andromeda of the bog—chained to an uneasy habitat, to the long winter and the short summer—is doomed never to be rescued because to be rescued would mean death to this particular botanical Andromeda.

The Cassandra in particular formed a low hedge at the place where the bog dropped off into the open water. As we paddled past in the boats, the bushes stood higher than our heads, for the bog was nearly two feet thick, sheer above open water. In the depths we could see the vague murkiness of ancient, saturated peat and a tangle of roots. The Cassandra bushes helped to hold the edge secure. They had been growing here for perhaps half a century and although very old were still low in stature, with a gnarly, twiggy growth from a tangled root base, and small, oval, dark-green leaves.

When one of the men reached out and took hold of one of the bristly Cassandra bushes and tugged, the pull did not dislodge the

Cassandra

plant. It only shook the vegetation and the bog itself for yards around the bush and at the same time sent broad ripples out into the water. Solid though the filled-in muskeg looked, solid indeed with the compact matting of plants packed tightly together and all their roots interwoven in a compact fabric, there was no true soil or real stability. The vegetation was not really anchored anywhere, was still suspended several feet thick above open water.

We would have to come back in early June to see the Cassandra in bloom, all its bending twigs decorated with strands of closely set, pure-white pearl-bells shaped like the flowers of the bearberry. The Andromeda would also be in bloom with its pale-pink bells—but Andromeda would be noticeable at any time because of its unique, pale-pink upper stems and the pale-blue leaves. Not truly green at all, the leaves are almost a soft wedgwood blue instead. They are very narrow and rolled under to meet the chalky-white undersides.

PITCHER PLANTS

Never in my life had I seen so many pitcher plants as this tremendous acreage of muskeg afforded. Thousands must have been visible, each tall stem arched to hold one bent-over maroon flower three inches wide, or what remained of the flower. The blossoms themselves are purple-red in June, while the sun shining through the petals turns them a rosy-red on a bright day. Around the base of each cluster of tall flower stalks, the pitcher-shaped leaves make a heavy, buoyant platform. It is always difficult to photograph a close-up view of the whole pitcher plant because the flower is perched on the end of a foot-long stem above those low-lying red-and-green trumpets of leaves which are often half hidden as they lie back, half full of water, in the moss.

Even after the petals have fallen, the sturdy flowers retain their form and elegance all summer. The maroon sepals remain cupped in the form of the flower itself. All summer long the forming, ovoid seed capsule is sheltered by a five-pointed, umbrella-shaped bract fastened to the outer end of the pistil. Into this umbrella an insect must have had to scramble in order to get at the pollen and fertilize the pistil. By winter, when the sepals have shriveled down around the cherry-shaped seed capsule, the umbrella has curved up around its lower end and, in drying, is secured around it. The

Pitcherplant

five points just fit into the hollows between the sepals, thus nicely enclosing the whole thing for the winter. Quantities of small, pale-brown seeds, furrowed in little ridges and hollows, and about twice the size of celery seeds, are released inside this container. By spring many have been slowly scattered into the bog.

The pitcher plants, Sarracenia, seem admirably suited to a difficult and demanding environment. In a hungry habitat, they seem to be far from a state of starvation. They are well fed and must evidently thrive, if their numbers here are any indication of totally successful adaptation to difficult bog conditions. Because of the lack of available nitrogen, the carnivorous pitcher plant obtains its proteins from insects which it entraps in its inflated, specialized leaves. Some kinds of plants bait a trap and then close down on the victim. The pitcher plant simply holds up its attractive soup kettles and entices fresh meat to walk in and become an ingredient in a potent protein broth.

The leaf, unlike normal leaves, forms a funnel, tube, or cornucopia, as if the leaf had been rolled up and glued along its sides, making a neat wing or flange as a seam. A landing field is formed by the fluted opening of the pitcher as it bends back a little to make a lip. The whole curious structure tapers to a small point where the stem joints the cluster of many pitchers, large and small, at the root.

There are four distinct zones of entrapment on the leaf. First of all, it flaunts a color which is evidently attractive to flies—meat-red. Since there is also some nectar on the red veining of the leaf-opening, some botanists believe that it may be the nectar, rather than the red color, which attracts the fly. In any case, when an insect lands on this porch of decision, it finds the red veins leading to nectar, then moves along the crimson route in obvious delight, flirting its wings and lapping up the momentary treat. But the picnic ends on a glassy-smooth surface just where the pitcher suddenly starts down in a long curve.

Inside this receptacle the insect tumbles down a long, slippery slope which is carpeted with silky hairs all pointing below. This well-brushed shag rug sends a victim quickly to the bottom and restrains it from trying to clamber up again. In a swoosh, the victim is dumped into the pot of "soup" at the bottom—water containing a digestive enzyme. In it are the odorous remains of previously caught insects, now pretty well digested, and the residue decaying in a slimy black mass. The best-fed pitcher plants, it seems, have the foulest smell of carrion. Those whose pitchers are filled to the brim with clean rain water have little odor, and until the water level drops in each pitcher and the concentrated enzyme gets to work on the meat products again, there is little food for the plant.

Occasionally an enterprising insect may try to gnaw its way out of the side of the pitcher and sometimes succeeds in escaping, but this must happen very seldom. Most are successfully caught, and the pitcher plant is nourished on a broth whose solution is strong enough to kill and disintegrate most insects.

There are, of course, certain insects which must find a challenge in outwitting any menace, and so some have even managed to live in the potent fluid inside the pitcher. A mosquito of the bogs has overcome the menace of the enzyme and actually lays its eggs in the water of the pitcher. The young wigglers frisk about in a brew which would kill another kind of insect less hardy. The larvae hatch into adults which depart to lay their own eggs in other pitchers in the bog.

The mosquito is not the only one to triumph over the power of Sarracenia. A small fly lays its eggs in the mass of carrion in the bottom of the pitcher. The white larvae feed on the dead material supplied to them by the plant. They mature as small flies which are instrumental and necessary in the cross-pollination of the pitcher-plant flowers. Turn about, in this case, is certainly fair enough play, in unwittingly repaying one benefit with another—by not eating the fly, the plant is fertilized. By fertilizing the plant, the fly unknowingly insures an unending supply of pitchers in which to lay its eggs.

THE BOG

Two other creatures—and perhaps more—also use the pitchers for their own ends. Certain spiders often spin webs just inside the opening. They catch insects before they have a chance to reach the deadly liquid below. And a small wasp makes a little raft on the water inside the container on which to lay her eggs.

The world of the bog is the world of carnivorous plants. Aside from the big pitcher plants, there were the golden-flowered bladder-

Bladderwort

worts, the Utricularia, and two species of tiny sundews, Drosera. That morning it seemed to me that there were so many upheld pitchers, so many outstretched, clutching, sticky little palms of the sundews, so many open-mouthed pouches of the bladderworts—the whole area seemed hungry! We needed to get out on to the bog itself to investigate its occupants more fully than we could from the boats. After paddling slowly along the rim of the bog and poking in as far as we could go into the overgrown, boggy bays, we finally found a place to land. Not that it was really *land*—it was only a little entryway into the muskeg itself where we could pull in with the boats and tie up to a dead tamarack.

THE QUAKING BOG

Climbing from a rocking boat and getting out on to the uneasy foothold of the bog was something of a trick, like stepping on a soft and bouncy innerspring mattress. It was guaranteed to cause certain qualms as to where one's foot would eventually go. We could surmise something of the amount of ice water beneath the quaking bog; we knew that there were always lurking bottomless black holes in the fabric of moss which were part of the black and oozy peat muck below. Still, there was a fairly good place to get out, and by helping each other, assisted in turn by the conveniently placed trees as hand-holds, we managed to stand teetering on the quaking bog.

The very uneasiness of the place gave us an exciting sensation of traversing a vastly primitive landscape, which of course it is. You cannot civilize a bog without ruining it. This is the same kind of landscape which formed when the glaciers were melting, the same kind we now might find all the way beyond the tree line, to the Arctic Circle itself. The immediate muskeg which we were on (or in) stretched to our horizon to the north; it filled all the bays and curves to the east. It was a low-lying wilderness of sphagnum, laurel, Cassandra, Andromeda, stunted swamp spruces, dead tamaracks, and young live tamaracks. It was the world of the subarctic today.

The spruces and tamaracks both go north to the line of trees, becoming more and more stunted and punished, the farther northward they go, and they lean because of the lack of any solid rooting material. The tamaracks themselves perhaps once filled this bog.

Cycles of tamaracks come and go. Periodically the sawfly lays its eggs on the leaf-bud tips of well-grown tamaracks. Normally the sawfly larvae destroy a few buds and cause no widespread damage until one of their big years when there is a population explosion and a tremendous crop of caterpillars denudes whole trees of their needles. The trees frequently die that year or, weakened by the next year's infestation, perish soon afterward. It may seem a tragedy when the tamarack stand is destroyed; yet, in the economy of this tree, it has become a means of perpetuation. In the dense old tamarack swamp, the feathery young trees fail to grow for lack of light and air. When the old trees are killed, the young ones may have a chance to develop. This, however, is not always true when the swamp spruces move instead into the dying tamarack stand, com-

THE BOG

pletely replacing the latter. The tamaracks do not come back into the area, at least as a pure planting, until the spruces, in turn, are dying.

Bogs like this one, extending circumpolarly around the top of the world, are vital in holding water in suspension throughout the year rather than letting it flow away in a hurry during the times of melting snow or heavy rains. The bogs are indeed a vast, spongy reservoir. The whole upper portion of the continents would be a great deal drier and warmer, and no doubt much less snowy, without this tremendous acreage of liquid held in reserve and only slowly released. Consider the supply in the pitcher plants alone! One large pitcher may hold more than half a cupful of water, and there may be eight to a dozen pitchers on one plant. One pitcher plant, therefore, may hold nearly two quarts of liquid. And when I start to multiply pitcher plant numbers in one bog—!

But the hungry ones—we could not forget their presence. In a place where standing water was visible in the moss, the yellow flowers of the bladderworts, Utricularia, bobbed and danced in the wind. They were bonnet-shaped, almost pea-shaped, yet had a spur like that of a nasturtium. The slender stalks stood above the ferny, aquatic leaves which were down in the shallows. These submerged leaves were as dissected as the gills of a fish and were used for much the same purpose in filtering oxygen from the water. On their floating roots were many little bladders yawning for food.

Each helmet-shaped bladder was about an eighth of an inch long or less and was furnished with a tiny valvular lid in one end, there where various forking hairs and tentacle-like protuberances thrust forth. Apparently, when some tiny water creature enters the porch of the bladder, it stimulates the valve to open. This sudden inward movement causes a suction and a current which sweep the creature into the bladder. The long hairs prevent any escape from the current. Once inside, the insect, the daphnia, copepod, or diatom is trapped. The valve closes behind it—forever. The bladderwort evidently does nothing to kill its prey or actually to lure it to its death.

Simply crowding the victims until they suffocate readies the protein matter for an enzyme which reduces it to a state to be absorbed by the plant.

SUNDEWS

Of all the carnivorous plants in this place, the little sundews were surely the most abundant. They populated the sphagnum by thousands, by hundreds of thousands; yet, to glance over the bog, none could at first be seen. They were certainly a good deal more tiny than most of us ever expected them to be when we first saw their pictures in the botany textbooks.

Sundews are usually illustrated singularly with the much larger pitcher plant, the Venus flytrap, and other carnivorous plants. They are shown with very little true differentiation or comparative size. You seldom find just one sundew on a smooth place where its miniature size might stand out. Instead, they grow out of the rosettes of the sphagnum itself and produce rosettes in themselves. It takes a good deal of peering at the hummocky, wet jungle of the bog-moss to focus on them. The leaf whorl is seldom or never more than two inches in total width and is often half that size. They are large enough to be seen, and of course they were there all the time. But they are amazingly invisible until they are at last discovered. Then they seem to be quite everywhere.

The sundew puts up a long flower stalk which at first is curled over. Buds begin to open from the lower portion to the top, each brief blossom opening at the place where the uncoiling stem bends. Finally, the entire six-inch, wiry stalk stands erect with its forming seeds. There were two sundews in this place, the round-leaved and the intermediate, with the former the more abundant and the latter the one chiefly found growing at the very edge of water and hanging over the bog rim, or actually submerged in shallow water.

I suppose the only way really to see a sundew is to use a hand lens on its marvelous leaves. Each slender stem rising from the base —a stalk little more than an inch or so long—has a small disk leaf which may be an eighth to half an inch wide. This is set with thin tentacles, sometimes as many as two hundred and sixty. Each one is tipped with a gland which secretes a clear, sticky substance (which stains white paper pink) that glitters like dewdrops in the sunshine. Without the sparkle of this artificial dew, the sundew plants are more difficult to find. Early in the season when they were just uncoiling their tiny knots of leaves and had as yet produced no secretion, I had to peer nearsightedly at the multitudes of sphagnum rosettes in order to locate any sundews at all.

Drosera, the sundew, is a deadly little thing. As a plant, its concentration on catching animal life seems to be almost more than plantlike. The gland-tipped tentacles are extremely sensitive and have the power of responding to stimulus. The lightest touch of a living thing, a midge or a mosquito, causes the sundew leaf to react at once. Oddly, when the wind carries debris against the leaf, it does not respond. In finding what sundews would do and what they would take in, Darwin made numerous tests which must have exhausted both him and the sundews. He discovered that they reacted to almost every protein substance or animal matter, as well as to milk and to ammonia sulphate. Securing a small live fly half an inch away from the plant, he saw that it immediately started moving a leaf toward the insect and within two hours had not only reached but had touched and begun to engulf it.

The pressure of a gnat stopping on a filament causes a stimulus of protoplasm in the tentacle, which darkens visibly. Nearby tentacles are alerted; they start bending forward on the leaf, drawing the victim to the center where the shorter tentacles wait. These are green, while the tentacles on the rim are longer stemmed and are usually purplish or red.

In about an hour the insect it totally enclosed under tentacles from which is flooding a sticky, clear liquid which covers the prey. The secretion contains a powerful digestive fluid similar to pepsin in animal stomachs. As the secretion turns acid and ferments, the leaves are capable of true digestion and can even assimilate cartilage and tooth enamel. The glands absorb the dissolved matter through their bent-over tips pressed against it.

When a living insect is caught on a sundew leaf, the creature is generally dead within fifteen minutes, simply from suffocation. The dense secretion closes the insect's breathing apparatus. When the plant has digested the food, the tentacles uncurl and stand erect again. They are dry until the roots bring up enough water to supply the glands with more fluid, after which they are ready to catch another meal. The sundew's immediate need for having a reserve of water always available at the roots is its basic reason for growing in the bog. Perhaps the abundance of food is another reason.

Sundew

The insect-destroying potential in this plant must be really tremendous. If one small sundew leaf may catch as many as nine gnats —Charles Darwin counted thirteen on one leaf—think of how many gnats and mosquitoes might be slaughtered by a hundred-thousand sundews, each with eight to twenty leaves, growing all across that great wet haunt of the gnat, the mosquito, the no-see-um, in just this one bog! When I think of the thousands of similar, sphagnum-sundew bogs spread around the entire northern circumference of the world, the higher mathematics involved is staggering.

PINGUICULAS

There is another small northern carnivorous plant, related to the Utricularias rather than to the sundews, which I had found in the unlikely habitat of the grim shore rocks of upper Lake Superior.

Pinguicula

Expecting to find little more than the toughness of lichens on the rocks off Grand Marais, Minnesota, I came instead upon a strange and wonderful garden. It was composed of low, three-toothed cinquefoils with glossy, varnished leaves and white flowers growing in crevices in the rocks, as I had also found them growing in the high mountains; little purple and white lobelias and bright-blue harebells, as I had seen growing in the dunes much farther south; and some incredible golden-flowered bush cinquefoils of great beauty, like those I had come upon at Bierstadt Lake in Colorado, as well as in the Ridges.

There was one huge butter-and-eggs plant of magnificence and splendor, and lichens, of course, the brilliant orange rosettes of Xanthoria which grows where the gulls have perched. And there were the little, fragile-looking, pale lettuce-green rosettes of Pinguicula, one of the carnivorous plants. Tender though the little inch-long leaves might seem, they had survived very well in a habitat in which many plants might have quickly perished or never have attempted to grow at all. They jutted from crannies in the harsh, dark, purple-brown rocks, above rock pools, in exposed places upon which the storms of northern Lake Superior are flung in violence the year around, and where each winter the ice crowds in with great slabs and floes to engulf this shore.

Pinguicula (which deserves a nicer name; butterwort, another name, is not much better) has a violet-like, lavender flower on a short stem held above the leaves. The latter are covered with very fine hairs and a substance which makes them seem greasy to the touch. The narrowly oval leaves lie open, but the edges are slightly curled inward. They contrive to curl over still farther to engulf small insects which stop on the leaf. The greasy secretion from the leaves serves to kill and digest the prey.

In the great bog around Wolf Lake there were no Pinguiculas. The field was usurped by the other three floral carnivores, the animated sundews, the soup-pots of the pitcher plants, and the fish-traps of the bladderworts. They were all part of that unreal atmosphere of mystery which is part of the bog world. That quality of unreality also lies in the uneasy sensation of the stuff lying underfoot—stuff which isn't soil, and isn't water, yet is compounded of plants which are so solidly matted together that they bear the weight of a man above open water. The structure, made up of mosses and other plants in this dense, thick flooring, heaved as we walked on it. Yet, after the initial feeling of uneasiness, the experience became exhilarating. By distributing ourselves about on the quaking bog, twenty feet or so apart in all directions, and by starting the gentle heaving motion, we could shake the bog for an astonishing distance and set up responsive rings of ripples on the lake.

CANADA JAYS

As if to see what we were up to, a long-tailed gray-and-white bird flew in a long swooping flight and landed in one of the spruces nearby. The bird gave a quiet mewing sound and bent over to look down as we shook the bog. We stopped shaking and looked back at the bird. It had a puffy head with a black cap set well back, a short beak, and an engaging fluffiness and form which reminded us

Canada Jay

a good deal of an oversized chickadee. It was a Canada jay which had come to find out about us and, if possible, no doubt, to secure something to eat. It was joined by another, and another, until there were four big gray-and-white jays looking down at us. Hopping about in the bony branches of the scrawny spruce, they examined us from various angles.

We could offer them nothing. The lunch was back on the shore, and the cookies had long since been devoured.

Canada jays, or whiskey jacks, are birds of the spruce bogs, of the coniferous forests, of the subarctic. I enjoy them when they choose to follow along a trail with me. They parallel my course, pause when I pause. If I stop, they gather above in the branches and look down wistfully. They are delightful beggars.

The four had come from what appeared to be a pine island in the sea of muskeg. Perhaps long ago it really had been an island or a peninsula because there were enough sand and other substance for tall red pines to have found ample rooting. Around the rim of the island, just where it merged with the muskeg itself, lay a knee-high tangle of woody, curving, angular bushes clothed with narrow evergreen leaves which were thick and had rolled-under edges to meet a wool-covered underside. The upper leaves, the younger ones, had white wool; the older ones were furred with cinnamon-brown. We had come into the thickets of the Labrador tea, the merger between the wet bog and the slope up to the drier places.

Ledum, the tea (whose young leaves really do make a tea), is one of the splendid plants of the bog, a rhododendron whose thick,

Labrador tea

leathery leaves show its affinity with the more elaborate and larger members of that family in the south. Just now we found all the twig-tips set with conical brown buds about the size of a pea, and knew that from all these next spring would burst white bouquets with long protruding stamens. Then this rim of the bog becomes a flower garden of white, with the splendid lavender-pink flowers of the bog laurel in lovely contrast.

BOG LAUREL

Here and there, that summer day, we had found an aftermath flower or two of the laurel, Kalmia. Its cupped, fluted flowers are like those of the larger and only a trifle more elegant cousin, the mountain laurel, whose individual flowers are but little different in form or size. The blossoms of bog laurel are produced in smaller clusters, and certainly on much smaller plants than the mountain species—but perhaps the very insignificance of the stalks gives stature to the flowers. The sunshine glitters through their bright, silken, wine-pink cups, and the wind causes them to dance all across the rosy-painted bogs of June.

In the bud, the laurel is beautifully and crisply fluted in ten ridges to make a double cone which is broad around the middle and tapered at either end. On opening, the five points of the flower are held in a shallow cup, and in each of the ten ridges a stamen is pressed back as taut as a bowstring. The anther is held in a little tight pocket in the hollow; the narrow pistil stands out tall above all the bent-back stamens. When a small moth or tiny bee enters

Bog Laurel

the flower, the bent bows of the stamens are triggered by the slight pressure, and, leaping out of their sockets, they spring forward and plaster pollen on the insect. It carries the stuff along to the next flower, where some of it may be left on the pistil.

The leaves of the small bog laurel, unlike the often six-inch-long evergreen leaves of the mountain species, are seldom more than an inch in length, very narrow, bright, glossy, dark green (or vivid scarlet in autumn), rolled under to the white underside. This rolling is a customary habit in plants whose leaves must conserve moisture; it was, besides, no doubt the first step in the evolution of needles on coniferous trees.

The whole confection of a laurel plant is little more than a foot or two, often much less than that in the upper reaches of the tundra where it may be only a few inches tall. Yet it still holds the laurel splendor in its fluted pink flowers.

COTTONY SEDGE

We pushed through knee-high switches holding silken white plumes of cottony sedge, Eriophorum, the cotton-grass. To glimpse at a distance a sunny space dancing with white tufts at the ends of those slim whiplashes is to know at once that there is a sphagnum underpinning. The cotton-puffs, the bunny-tails, some toasty brown, some pure white, some in clusters of two or three silky white powderpuffs, some dangling like chenille tassels, are all part of the northern bog and the tundra. To see the growth here joins us immediately with all that tundra and bog terrain where curlews nest

Cottony Sedge

and white whales splash in the pale-blue waters of Hudson Bay. In the few places southward where cottony sedge is found, the familiar boggy underpinning left behind in isolated pockets when the Ice Age ended is at once identified.

WILD CALLA

We plunged unaware into a suddenly soggy place where green algae lay in masses of prehistoric-looking, gas-bubbled slime, where the wild callas grew. There were still some in bloom—oval white spathes with a crisp green spadix studded with yellow—above the heart-shaped, thick green leaves. But lying upon the wet moss around the pool were the fruits of the calla flowers which had blossomed in late May. The purple-red fruits looked rather like oversized mulberries three inches long and half that in thickness, their stems too weak to hold them upright. They proved their close kinship with the jack-in-the-pulpit in the woods with its similar, though bright-scarlet, seed clusters.

And then just as suddenly as we had been shoe-top deep in bog water where the callas grew, we stumbled over an ant-nest. Ants in a bog!

In the wilderness of the sphagnum, in a somewhat drier place among the Cassandra bushes, parched by the summer's sun, the ants had built a complicated structure two feet across and more than a foot high. They had used the dry sphagnum hummock itself, had carved their passageways and nurseries in the dessicated moss, had propped it up inside with bits of Cassandra stems and leaves. Then, as a finishing touch, the ants had neatly cut Cassandra leaves and had painstakingly laid them in a sort of loose upholstery all over the outside of the dome. The leaves did not hide or block any of the innumerable holes into and out of which the ants were coursing, as ants perpetually seem to do. Of all the oddities we found in the great bog, we had not expected to find enormous ant-nests, particularly abodes which utilized the sphagnum and Cassandra as these did. The ants themselves, black and shiny, went about their business as ants do on land.

There seemed to be little use that day in trying to find out how far the great bog with its dancing white bunny-tails and its ant colonies extended to the north. We could see that it curved around another headland, and realized that it might then continue for miles, perhaps even to the Gemini Lakes, those twin pools slowly being enclosed in bog. It was a tiring place in which to travel very far— that incessant sinking and pulling forth with a sucking, slushing sound, not really going in very far but not staying on top either. And having to climb over or go around the cranberry-strewn hummocks of muskeg with their bristling tufts of Cassandra was hard work.

As we started back to the boats, we walked a long way through cranberries growing over the fabric of the bog.

CRANBERRY COUNTRY

We had been seeing a great many wild cranberries in the moss, but not until we came back to the shore and set off in the boats around the edge of the bog (the long way around to the parking place), did we begin to get the full significance of that wild cranberry crop. None were yet ripe. They were almost fully grown, but would require another three weeks to a month to ripen; many of them were speckled red or were turning pink on one pale cheek. Although there were cranberries everywhere, they seemed to be most abundant along the margin where the open water began. Now we passed a continuous border of them, some bobbing in the cold

Wild Cranberry (LEFT)
"Moss-berries" (RIGHT)

water, some dangling close to it, the rest laid in festoons of slender plants over the moss.

Several varieties of cranberries grew here. Our guidebooks did not distinguish them by means of what seemed to be obviously variable characters of the fruit. There were at least two principal kinds, and we suspected there might be hybrids. Little dry vines with tiny leaves like miniature hemlock needles were laid like embroidery over hummocks of moss—the little European cranberries which are circumpolar, native to bogs all around the top of the world. The fruits were about half the size of the American cranberries which hung over the edges and dangled their cherry-round or oval or barrel-shaped fruits in the cold water. But there was a third cranberry smaller than either of these, which had minute vines laid on the moss—four-inch vines bearing one or two tiny, speckled fruits which were seldom red, but had freckles, the bits of the dark red-brown pigment remaining separated to make a brown-spotted fruit. Moss-berries, the commercial growers call them. Mingled with wild cranberry sauce later on, they were indistinguishable in flavor from the others. The cultivated species are derived from the large wild American cranberry.

Two of our number lived only a few hours drive from the bog. In October, long after the rest of us had gone home to more southern towns, these two went cranberrying. It was cold. The water was nearing the freezing point; the wind was icy; the berries were dead ripe. The pair scrambled through chill sphagnum now turned deep red in its autumn color, and they succeeded in gathering several pounds of mixed wild cranberries which were sent to me by special delivery. They were of many shapes, those choice muskeg fruits—squat, ovoid, oblong, round, with the little speckled moss-berries scattered as accent among them. That wild cranberry sauce—it was superb! It contained something of the essence of the bog and a memory of that day when some of the secrets of Wolf Lake were revealed.

On that summer day in the bog, we had started back with the

THE BOG

south wind in our faces, waves slapping the boats, and the hordes of pitcher plants standing above the bog, the spruce swamp calling, the distant pine-covered, gravel hills marking what once must have been the shore of the lake. We had come back at last to the one place where there was no bog, had tied up the boats, and made a fire to cook our lunch.

A loon went over, crying. The bird of the north was a link between solid land and the shaky footing of the bog. We had indeed come back to more familiar things, to a place where plants were plants and didn't eat animals, where land was firm and didn't quake and sink at every step, where moss grew in the woods and didn't render out half a cup of water when squeezed like a dishcloth. The world of dry land was a different world and way of life, yet in many ways it was dependent upon the world of the bog for its existence here. The land would be the reliable and solid place, slowly growing as a sequence of life out of the pioneering of the bog itself. But the bog, with its mystery and its reserve water and life, would always be the source, and it would always call to us with a voice that would not be denied.

CHAPTER SIX

ADVENTURES WITH ORCHIDS

I F we had visited the big muskeg in June, we not only would have found pink cranberry blossoms laced over the hummocks and dangling over the rim, and the dark-red flowers of marsh cinquefoil, but would have found certain orchids. The majority of the northern orchids come earlier than August, so that perhaps only the stately and splendid spires of the purple-fringed orchis, the small, fragrant ladies' tresses, and the rattlesnake plantain orchids, and few others, might be found in bloom so late in the season. But in May and June, the splendor of the orchid world comes alive in the presence of remarkable blossoms which seem to be more than flowers, to embody more than botany in their intricate structures and their intangible aura of mystery.

Showy Lady's Slipper

ADVENTURES WITH ORCHIDS

Perhaps it is the challenge of personal search and discovery, the mystery and the lure which send some of us on long hunts simply for the sight of a particular orchid. We are not like the plant hunters of the jungles who must collect their prey. We need not pick a flower in order to enjoy it, and we specifically do *not* pick orchids, those rarities which may perish as a species if collected too much. Orchid hunters of the northern places simply want to find that special flower, alone and wild and surrounded with its inexplicable air of unreality and aloofness, standing in its own private haunt of bog or swamp or forest. I suppose if orchids grew in ordinary places and were common to any roadside or woods, they would lose some of the allure which is so much a part of them. The quest is the thing, and the rarity. The search for an orchid may last all of our lives and take us into some of the most remote and splendidly wild areas in the land, and it will certainly contrive to get our feet wet in some of the choicest bogs on the continent.

In my youth I pored over a book called *Bog Trotting for Orchids*, by G. G. Niles, and another called *Our Wild Orchids*, by Morris and Eames. Both books are long out of print, but their contagion of excitement in hunting for orchids infected me then as now with an incurable enthusiasm of the most pleasant proportions. Part of the challenge, of course, came because I lived in a part of the country in which few wild orchids were still native, and so the longing to hunt for them became a consuming one, as much for the flowers as for the wilderness itself.

The very title of *Bog Trotting for Orchids* was a pleasure to think about. Knowing now, as I do, the amount of downright slogging and sloshing one does in a sphagnum bog, I cannot see how anyone, orchid hunting or not, may manage to *trot* in a bog. Nevertheless, the title is one which has sent more than one person into marshy haunts to hunt for orchids. Such people form a unique brotherhood to whom a northern peat bog presents an immediate challenge to enter and explore. To these kindred souls, the finding of a new bog plant—and most particularly a new orchid—is something to put glory in the day and a glow in the remembering.

It is not true of course that all wild orchids grow in bogs, any more than it is true that all tropical orchids perch in trees. Orchids, both northern and tropical, are noted for their extraordinary lack of conformity both in habitat and in shape and for their unique reproductive systems and strange flower forms which are part of that complex apparatus.

In hunting for orchids, we must at once forget that common conception of the species as resembling only the Cattleya or the Cymbidium pinned to the shoulder of the formal gown, or the lady's-slipper orchid of the woods. On any good day in orchid country, the astonishing pattern-variations are proved. A long perusal of a botany manual illustrating the great diversity of wild orchids is one of the best ways in which to fix their designs in the mind so that they may be recognized when they are found. To come upon one of these unreal flowers standing poised, without sound, without movement, perhaps almost invisible until it is focused upon, is a great experience out of doors.

Although orchids are sometimes unpredictable, as everything in nature may sometimes be, they usually follow a certain pattern of habitat, each kind in its own chosen haunt and seldom deviating from the general order. I can perhaps no more expect to find the splendid yellow-fringed orchis where the white-fringed grows, or the coral-root orchids where the white lady's-slippers grow, than I can find showy orchis with showy lady's-slippers. There is no haphazard jumble. There is order in orchids.

They are scattered over much of the country. I have found those splendid spikes of the yellow-fringed orchis along roadsides of Georgia and Florida; the tall spires of the purple-fringed orchis in sandy, marsh roadsides of northern Wisconsin and Michigan; tiny brownie-slippers on the Bear Lake Trail, above nine thousand feet in the Rocky Mountains; Calypsos along the tumbling descent of Fall River in Colorado; the putty-root orchid on a glacial moraine in central Illinois; ladies' tresses in hard, dry clay in the broiling-hot

September sunshine at the rim of a midwestern woods; and pink moccasin flowers in the chill, shadowy, wet habitat of the sphagnum bog in spring. It is here in the haunt of the bog and the coniferous forest that some of the finest wild orchids in the country may be found—found with luck and a certain perseverance.

Orchids are part of that great habitat which was all part of the sequence of growth after the Ice Age ended. The natural successions of land from barren, wet sand to dark, moist forest formed much of the terrain most favorable for the growth of orchids. They throve largely in acid peat or in sand in coniferous regions where they found certain soil fungi required for their growth. These mysterious mycorrhizal fungi are apparently essential to the life and growth of all orchids. Before the presence of these organisms was realized or understood, it was usually impossible to grow tropical orchids in greenhouses, especially from seed, and hence the price of the blossoms was prohibitive. Orchid plants all had to be shipped to the florists and greenhouses. By understanding something of the role of the root fungi, the mystery of what they needed for life was solved—although perhaps not really understood—and orchids, thereafter, could be grown from seed in quantities large enough to turn them into a big business.

In transplanting the wild orchids, the great difficulty is in assuring the plants of a continuing supply of their vital soil fungi. Except in a very few species, transplanting is seldom very successful; or, if successful for a year or so, ultimate failure comes about when the fungi brought with the transplanted roots are finally exhausted.

Soil fungi form a network of threads on the tips of the orchid roots, and send hair-fine tubes into the roots themselves. They do it also on some tree roots as well as on those of the heaths, gentians, and certain other plants, most frequently on those which grow in areas of poor nourishment, acidity, and lack of nitrogen. The fungus obtains carbon-containing compounds from the host plant, and in turn makes nitrogen available to it. The situation is an intricate one of mutual benefit. As the carnivorous plants get their nitrogen in their own way, or as the lichens obtain theirs from places where birds have roosted, so do the orchids find their vital nitrogen in the activity of fungi on their roots. In so doing, they survive in some of the hungrier portions of the wild.

Ages ago the orchids were lilies. They had the regulation six parts of the lily flower. In some strange series of changes, certain species began to evolve into their present complex and diverse forms, until the family of orchids now contains some five hundred genera and more than twenty thousand species. Their flowers, instead of standing upright as the simpler lilies did, were tipped forward so that they faced outward. With the shift in position, problems in pollination had to be solved by changing the symmetry of the flowers—a bilateral symmetry instead of the radial symmetry of lilies. Sliced lengthwise, the orchid flower's parts were evenly divided; crosswise, not.

In the orchid, three similar sepals are colored like the petals. Below these is a third petal which is conspicuously colored, often boat-shaped, or spurred, or fringed, or pouched, called the lip. It often forms a trough to contain nectar with which to attract insects. In the lady's-slipper, the lip has become a large, ornamental pouch. In the Calopogon, no doubt just to be different, the flower has been turned upside down so that the lip is above, not below.

Since orchids are unable to fertilize themselves, they are thus entirely reliant upon specific kinds of long-tongued insects, particularly certain small bees. In each variety of orchid there is, in consequence, a means of attracting those necessary insects. It is done with a mechanical nicety, a precision of timing, design, and aim which are as commanding of awe as the shape of the flower itself—and the outward shape is only the means to the vital end, which is fertilization and the formation of seeds. Gorgeous or not, awe-inspiring or not, the orchid's only mission in life, after all, is to perpetuate itself.

The whole form of the blossom has thus been arranged to attract only certain insects and to keep out or send away unrewarded all others. All but the lady's-slipper have been refined down to one modified stamen, but that one stamen—or the two as in the lady's-slipper—concentrates its pollen and its powers in a marvelous way.

In each orchid this plan is different, but basically it is this: the pollen, instead of being scattered indiscriminately or picked up on any insect venturing in, is contained in little sacs called pollinia. On contact with insects which follow the orchid's orderly plan of entry and exit, the pollinia are plastered on head or thorax or back and carried intact to another orchid of the same species. (I once triggered this same mechanism unwittingly when I touched my finger to the rostellum of Cycnoches, the tropical green swan orchid, and found the pollinia suddenly ejected and glued securely to my finger.)

LADY'S-SLIPPERS

The lady's-slippers, *Cypripedium*, evidently are built to attract and fit small bees, and the whole mechanism of the flower is thus geared to just this one kind of insect. The flower is built to engender stock responses in the insect at each stage of its visit to the intricate structure. There must be something to attract the bee—color. And there must be a place to land—the curving lip or landing field of the pouch. Something must serve to draw its attention into the pouch—hence the nectar on fine, downy hairs in the bottom. Then the insect must be led to an exit which is different from the door by which it entered. It is and must be different because the bee on its way out must contact the pollinia and carry them away, and at the same time leave on the waiting stigma some pollen from a flower previously visited.

For a bee to leave without fulfilling any of its obligations would be a difficult feat because of the inrolled edge of the lip on the lady's-slipper, or the one-way-in slit in the pink moccasin which permits no exit. Still, in order that the small green bee does not become confused and try to go out the same way by which it entered, the bee must be led to go out the right way. There are, therefore, two little windows high up in the back of the flower, just beyond the two stamens with their pollinia, and placed behind the stigma. The bee scrambles up the slope in the rear of the flower—because it must—just touching the bent-over stigma and leaving pollen on it. Then the insect, still following the built-in orders from the flower, climbs past the two stamens, carries off their pollinia stuck to its head and back, and, following the light in the little windows, escapes with mission accomplished.

Thus the bee may actually be called the creator of the orchid pattern. Yet, did the bee adapt to the orchid design, or did nature arrange the flower to fit the bee? There are no records of fossil orchids, although this does not mean that there were none. There may have been, however, for some of these same orchid-pollinating bees have been found encased in amber which is dated at some seventy million years ago.

The showy lady's-slipper, a glorious, glistening, waxen white flower with a deep-pink blotch on the toe, is host to a tiny, metallic green bee which is no more than an eighth of an inch wide and five-sixteenths of an inch long. It just fits the mechanism of the flower and its little exit windows. Larger insects which venture in are caught between the sticky anthers and die there, unable to escape. To those legal bees which find their way inside the glistening pouch, the lady's-slipper provides only meager sips of nectar. The visitor is never filled to the brim. Appetite only whetted, the green bee then goes quickly to the next orchid for more nectar; thus, while the pollen is fresh, it is carried to where it belongs.

It would be a sorry thing if everything desirable out of doors had been found and there were no more quests. There are fortunately enough wild orchids in America to provide a source of botanical adventure for many years, for few of us manage in one lifetime to find them all.

In the Ridges Sanctuary, thirty orchid species have been found.

ADVENTURES WITH ORCHIDS

This today is remarkable, yet it is an indication of what the wilds must have held before draining, burning, grazing, lumbering, and civilizing ruined many parts of the landscape for the specialized growth of orchids and kindred rarities. There once were thousands of white lady's-slippers in the old Calumet marshes where the steel mills and railroad yards of South Chicago and Gary, Indiana, now conceal all traces of clean earth and bog. Orchids elsewhere were often in great abundance in the wilderness areas which are now gone. To find them today is to glimpse the past, for the orchid holds more of that essence of wilderness in its blossoms than many other flowers which may adapt more readily to the encroachments of civilization.

Knowing this, the sight of almost three hundred yellow lady's-slippers in one small patch of maple woods on a May day was enough to set me back on my heels in wonder, delight, and disbelief. In these days, orchids just don't come in those numbers, or only so rarely that the occurrence is truly a cause for marveling. I had found my first yellow lady's-slipper in sloping, dryish, rocky woods in Indiana, one here, one there, not more than half a dozen in all. Then I found no more until, many years later, I came into those sunny spring woods in northern Wisconsin and found this burst of golden bloom which must have been something like that of the primitive past. There they were, most of their waxen slipper-pouches facing around to the south where the sun came into the woods. Their russet ties and sepals flared almost red in the afternoon light. These were not single specimens. They grew in clumps, sometimes as many as thirty together from one root. Standing in one spot and slowly pivoting while I counted, I tallied 289 yellow lady's-slippers within immediate view, and I knew there were many more beyond.

From the evidence of many mature pods, splitting to release their infinitely fine dust of seeds, there must have been a good many little green bees last year visiting the slippers and behaving in the proper manner to effect pollination. Perhaps as important was the fact that these woods had been protected from fire, cutting, and grazing for more than a quarter of a century, so that a nucleus of orchids had had a chance to multiply freely, unhindered and undestroyed.

The showy lady's-slipper—that most elegant wild orchid and the tallest of the lady's-slippers—was a good deal more elusive. Yet, in a sunny opening an arbor vitae swamp, I came upon them suddenly, almost casually, on a bright day in June. Three feet tall, each stalk bearing two to four large, waxen white slippers with that glowing purple-pink on the toe, they caught the light and glistened with the jewel-dust sparkle which some flowers possess. This sparkle is caused by a thin surface layer of cells which are transparent and, like a multitude of tiny mirrors, reflect light.

There were wood lilies burning pure orange-red in the open places; there were Indian paintbrush and white camas, and there would be hosts of grass-of-Parnassus and gentians later on; but the mystery of these showy lady's-slippers produced a strange awe which the others would not. I could see now why some orchid hunters in the tropics had been so bemused by what they had found, how the Spanish priests in Mexico could use the Holy Dove orchid to tell the story of the Trinity, how blue Vandas, white moth orchids, spider orchids, golden Turrialbas, and leopard Cymbidiums might create superstition and fear among native and white man alike. The mystery was here in these silent flowers cupped lightly in my hands.

The pink moccasin flower, one rosy blossom on a stem that rises from a pair of deeply ribbed, downy leaves which may grow from a hummock of damp peat moss, contains some of this same air of mysticism, and there is that other one—not a lady's-slipper—the calypso, which holds a curious allure. Calypso was the nymph who ensnared Ulysses and held him willingly captive for seven years on her magical island of Ogygia.

CALYPSO

My own search for Calypso had been pursued vainly for many years. Whenever I was in the nymph's northern neighborhood I

Calypso

had hunted. To begin with, though, I was really looking in the wrong places. I had thought—no doubt had read carelessly in the orchid books—that such a little rarity must necessarily grow in a bog. I had therefore been hunting in wet places of the north country without a particle of luck. Bog after bog had left me thwarted. In the heaving, hazardous stretches of many a quaking bog I wandered and plunged. I found rose pogonia and early coral-root and the charming pink butterflies of the upside-down Calopogon. I finally came upon the splendid and mysteriously alert-looking Arethusa standing with satyr's ears upright, listening as if for something I could not hear. There were no Calypsos.

I could not wade through bogs forever. Dry paths were pleasant for a change. I knew all too little about the great forest of virgin white pine and hemlock, with its scattering of mountain maple and white birch, its fountaining ferns and thick mosses which carpeted stretches of earth, as well as every log and rock. Here in late May I came upon the leafless, rose-russet, stalks of striped coral-root orchids. They were in clusters and clumps like some strange sort of ruby asparagus, with no green at all (they are saprophytes on dead material in the soil). Their translucent, sparkling, pink, maroon, and white blossoms twisted from the smooth stems and caught the sunlight. There were the small, fragile, green-gold, early coral-roots too, delicate as something created in wax. Buds were coming on the clintonias, and the tiny amber froth of snowflake-shaped flowers were appearing on the small plants of bishop's cap. But there were no Calypsos here.

It was the first day of June when I took the mossy trail into an old cedar forest which lay on the far side of the pine woods. I heard the loud cackling and drum-beat thumping of a pileated woodpecker hacking on a tree somewhere in the distance. A cedar is stout of fiber and its wood is one of the most extraordinarily tough to be found in the north; yet, the big black, red, and white, crow-sized woodpecker, the log cock, seems to delight in chiseling precision-built boxes in the living wood, gouging deeply into the white heartwood itself.

The woods were quiet again. Not even a chickadee called, nor was a red squirrel sounding his alarm to challenge and announce my coming. When the squirrels rattle out the news, I might as well come with fife and banner, for all the secrecy I can maintain. But now the forest was still. The very brooding green-darkness of the arbor vitae insisted upon reverence, a silence to fit their own silence, an awe to match the forest's incomparable antiquity and mystery.

At the base of a large arbor vitae beside the deer trail I found where another woodpecker had been working only that morning. The dark earth and moss were littered with huge, fresh, snowy chips three inches long, flung out from an excavation which the bird must have made by sitting on the ground. He had hacked a space almost eight inches wide and four inches deep in the base of the tree, as if the bird expected, with reasonable diligence, to cut it down. A fine start certainly had been made on the project.

And just around the curve of trunk there stood a small, silent, pink flower with a strange glow around it—there stood the Calypso orchid. The woodpecker had led me to the nymph.

One flower on a six-inch stem, one oval, corded leaf lying back on the russet carpet of fallen arbor vitae needles—the simplicity and the grandeur of this small pink entity were overwhelming to a strange degree. The open, rose-colored little slipper was intricately veined with purple and white, and furred with gold on the lip. Pink sepals and petals stood above the flower like the four little ribbons to tie the slipper to a fairy's foot. In another interpretation of its appearance, and because of the clean line resembling a jawbone and head and upraised antlers to be imagined in the shape of the flower, the Calypso is sometimes called deer's head orchid. The stance of the blossom has a curiously eerie sort of listening attitude, as the Arethusa has with its satyr's ears. Perhaps of all the flowers which I have found and have wondered about, none had the effect upon me of that single Calypso at the base of a tree on which a woodpecker had hewn in mighty strokes a signboard to discovery.

A further exploration of the woods beyond resulted in finding a dozen more, each Calypso quite alone, each one standing at the base of the tree. However, I know that they may be found in clumps and groups, and that there often are white forms—none, I am sure, ever to be quite as exciting as that first one in the cedar wood.

Other orchids grow in the deep woods, but their time of blossoming is spread from May to September. Summer is a low period, yet it is the time to look for the Hooker's orchis with its pairs of water-lily-shaped leaves laid back on the moss and a tall spike of green flowers rising between. The Hooker's orchis is not as splendid in color as many species, but the form of the individual flower when examined is as intricate as any, its spurs or "hooks" helping me to remember the name.

In August in the pine woods there grow small white orchids on slim spikes which rise above miniature rosettes of reticulate-veined, green-and-white leaves, the rattlesnake plantain orchids. They seldom set their few, small, white roots into the soil. Rather, the plant grows on a loose mat of old pine needles. Here live the fungi which are necessary to the life of this orchid. The fungus is on the

Rattlesnake Plantain

pine needles themselves when they fall—and here below the trees the rattlesnake plantain, Goodyera, is usually to be found. It can be picked up easily from its light rooting in the needles. Its flower stem is three to five inches tall and bears white-furred, hooded white blossoms.

LADIES'-TRESSES

Along woodland trails or under pines and beside the roads in summer and early autumn, sometimes in dry, exposed, unlikely places, I have come upon the slender, wiry, fragrant spires of

Ladies'-Tresses

ladies'-tresses orchids and have smelled their wonderfully sweet, vanilla perfume. No, not all are vanilla-flavored. The power of distinction in a fragrance is an aid to identifying some of the ladies'-tresses, for one of them may smell like vanilla—*Spiranthes cernua*—and another like almonds—*Spiranthes Romanzoffiana*. The ladies'-tresses flowers are white, waxen, fringe-lipped little bonnets which are arranged in a sort of braided spiral around the stem. Those of the slender ladies'-tresses are only about half the size of the others. The tiny white blossoms with a green line on the lip appear to be neatly wound on the stalk and, although so tiny, are splendid under a lens.

These orchids, small as they are, invite specialized insects to enter, help themselves, and depart with pollen. The ladies'-tresses flower has a little trough of nectar in front as a landing field and lure, and the insect, in bending forward to sip, brushes the rostellum. This is the structure, usually in the top of the flower, which holds the pollinia and the pistil. In ladies'-tresses, the rostellum has in its center a narrow, boat-shaped disk containing a sticky liquid. It is covered with a thin membrane which is easily ruptured by the force of the insect pushing headlong against it. After this is broken, a sticky fluid glues itself to the tongue of the bee and the boat-shaped disk is pulled out, along with the pollinia themselves. The plastered bee flies off with its load.

CALOPOGON

Another orchid tosses out any bee or other insect which attempts to land. The bee tribe evidently hasn't the sense to take a hint and try less inhospitable flowers, for they come back again and again

Calopogon

to the Calopogon. The kind which is especially attracted to and necessary for pollination of this species—those charming pink butterfly-orchids of the open, sunny, tamarack bog—evidently cannot distinguish clearly the pink color of the flower itself but focuses instead on the golden fur of the lip. In most orchids, the lip lies where it traditionally belongs, in the lower part of the flower. But in the Calopogon, as mentioned earlier, it is placed above rather than below, because the flower itself is actually inverted. Nearsightedly, the bee heads for the attractive golden fringe and lands clumsily upon it because there is no landing field where one is customarily located. The bee's weight immediately pulls down the fringed lip with the insect clinging to it, and dumps it on its back on the rostellum just below. The kicking bee is cradled briefly in its curve; the glue gland breaks and pours glue and pollen on the bee's furry back. It is over in a moment. In some confusion, the bee recovers itself; it departs without having obtained anything to eat for its trouble—then forgetfully is attracted to another lovely and inhospitable Calopogon flower. Here, as it does the same thing, it manages at the same time to plaster pollen in the right spot for fertilization before making off with a fresh supply newly applied with orchid glue. The Calopogon's efficient dumping system works very well.

All these devious orchid mechanisms, which of course are not operated knowingly or with any conscious plan, help to give that quality of strangeness to this mysterious tribe, product of bogs and swamps and roadsides, of woods and mountains and tundra. They teach of wilderness, of soil fungi, and convey at the same time some of the strange magic of the orchids on our landscape.

CHAPTER SEVEN

THE CONIFEROUS FOREST

THE actions of my light meter were perhaps the best indication of what was happening. Out on the open beach the meter had registered its highest figure, so that in taking pictures of blowing beach grass or of cinquefoil embroidery, the lens of the camera had had to be shut to its smallest aperture. As I walked inland, at first through the lightly wooded ridges and openings and swales, the lens had had to be opened wider at each reading. Just as the camera found less light and must literally have its eye opened wider in order to see what must be photographed, so also had the vegetation changed in adapting itself to the dimmer light.

Among the aspens and young firs and pines, the light was of

medium strength. The meter now registered 8. This was the place called Wintergreen Ridge where the Canadian carpet was at its best and where the arbutus bloomed every spring. As soon as I crossed the swale to Deer Lick Ridge, the light reading dropped suddenly to 5.6. When, later on, I was under the pines and hemlocks, and then beneath cedars, it was 3.5 in the very lightest places, 1.5 in the hemlock wood, and considerably less than that where the trees were most dense and old and the light was at its minimum.

The varnished, waxed, or Venetian-blind leaves of the outer beach were no longer here. In the shade, the principal need of leaves was not protection from light, but a means of taking in as much of it as possible from the small supply which managed to filter through the uppermost canopy of trees. Leaves must be broad and thin to take advantage of every vestige of sunlight, or must be needle leaves. They must also be able to live in a shade that would destroy many kinds of plants. It was not only a place for the coniferous trees, but for the thin leaves of moosewood and maple-leaved viburnum, for ferns, for mosses, for thimbleberries with their big, beautiful, star-shaped leaves and their white wild-rose-like blossoms.

The realm of the old pines and hemlocks was a dark, strange, and wonderful place. The great trees in this virgin tract, where none had ever been logged and where the dead trees had fallen to the forest floor to build up a soft and spongy humus, was a completely different world. The whole structure was geared to the lack of light. Only where a tree had fallen had the light been permitted to come in. However, this meager opening often gave enough sunlight to

Balsam Fir

permit seedlings of birches and aspens to grow. They seemed like outsiders among the splendid dimensions of pines and the dark veilings of the hemlocks, with the burnished brass bark of the shade-tolerant yellow birches, all very ancient and hoary with mosses and mushrooms, with lichens and liverworts and moss. Yet, it is through this letting in of light by the falling of a tree or of many trees that the whole forest is ultimately changed and renewed. When it has become a climax forest—which means that the fully grown trees have made so much shade that no new seedlings are able to grow beneath or among them—there is then no further progress except for that of destruction and of starting all over again.

THE CLIMAX FOREST

If the climax forest remained unchanged it would eventually die in its entirety when all the trees had reached their final age limit and expired. In the lack of light, even pine and hemlock seedlings fail to grow, and because of this same situation no trees from outside can come in. But in nature nothing remains static for very long. No situation endures for the permanent harm of the place. There is always change, always transition, always the continuity of life. As nature abhors vacuums, bare places, and monotony, so it must also abhor a static condition in which nothing is happening.

Nature never seems to want for ample ingenuity or resources to relieve any sort of condition. The original great pine forests of North America, extending for miles without interruption except for water-courses and occasional meadows and marshes and lakes, were never static. There was that continual slow change—and change need not be fast to accomplish its goal of renewal. Nature has all the time in the world. Change may take a moment, an hour, a day, a year, a century, an eon. What seems like permanence to us is only something which is undergoing a long, slow change which often extends far beyond our lifetime, while transience is change undergone quickly as we watch it. But it is all change, all with its interlocking purposes and its long-range goals.

Thus, in the old forests whose passing we lament—feeling as we do that we are solely responsible for their loss, and in a measure we are—there also was death and disaster. There was always change. Perhaps a pine died of borers or was hit by lightning, was weakened by fungi and carpenter ants and woodpeckers, and it fell, carving a corridor in the dark forest round about and perhaps taking other trees down with it as it crashed. Light came in, vital light which could foster a whole new plant succession. Successions in the old forest had gone as far as they would go—from open sand to sand-holders, to aspens and birches and firs, to beech-maple or to a climax forest of pine and hemlock. The only change now would be to start over, and letting in light would do this quicker than anything.

As if waiting for the opportunity, the wind-borne seeds of aspen and white birch start to grow. Shadbush or serviceberry trees are soon dancing with white flowers and amber-red leaves in spring and are hung with purple-red fruits to feed the bears and robins in August. Wild cherry trees spring up, too, and are white in spring—bird cherry and chokecherry, relishing a sudden opening with plenty of sunshine. Wild raspberry seeds, brought by birds, start the bushes to growing in the strip-clearing cut by the fallen tree.

After a while, in the fluttery shade of aspen and birch, there may be balsam fir seedlings. Eventually the birches and aspens, now old trees, their work done, die out. No new ones replace them because now the shade is again too great. In the protection of the towering balsams, there may come more pine seedlings and then hemlocks. The opening has long since grown closed again.

Often, instead of a return to coniferous trees, the long narrow openings left by fallen trees will foster the growth of hardwood trees—aspen, red maple, paper birch, basswood, then yellow or black birch, and sugar maple and beech. Thus, as the oldest pines and hemlocks continue to die and fall and let in sunlight, the entire aspect of what was for several hundred years a dark and majestic pine-hemlock forest may have slowly changed to a hardwood forest. In other places the return may again swing back to pines.

THE CONIFEROUS FOREST

In the Rocky Mountains, the Engelmann spruce forests are frequently infested and finally killed by the bark beetle. In the greater light let into the dying spruce forest, the alpine firs enter, and finally, when the spruces are all dead, the area has become a fir forest. But the firs are subject to attack by the balsam bark beetle. As the cycle of ruin comes to the alpine firs and they die, the area again is open to the return of the Engelmann spruce—a cycle which has been taking place ever since the end of the Ice Age.

It is a well-ordered plan for variation which keeps an area from remaining static and perhaps depleting nutrients in the soil. In a grand scale of crop rotation, nature rotates its woodlands—brings maples and beeches into a dying pine forest, and, when the cycle of the hardwoods may be finished some hundreds of years hence, may bring in more pines and hemlocks or some other group of trees in a logical sequence.

In the western coniferous forests there may be a few lodgepole pines in a fir-spruce forest. When a fire sweeps crackling through the highly inflammable firs and spruces, and the lodgepole pines explode in great torches of flame, and the area is then left stark and horrid in the charred, rain-soaked aftermath of the fire, the cones of the lodgepole pine begin to open and release their seeds. It takes a fire to do it. When the fire passes, it is the lodgepole pine which has begun to reforest what once was a tract of fir and spruce. As the pines eventually die of age, it is the fir and spruce which usually come back. In northern bogs, when the tamaracks are killed by sawfly infestations, the black or swamp spruces move back. As they age and die, it is the tamaracks which usually return.

Everywhere there is a continuous change, of one kind of habitat superceding another when the latter's guard is down or when some change comes to weaken it. A meadow is constantly being encroached upon by the marching seedlings of trees from the nearby woods, ranks of them following behind the pioneering aspens which start out in the front.

In the same way, the marsh cannot remain forever a marsh. If

Spartina grass is present, the marsh may turn into a wet prairie, then eventually into a dry prairie, and later it may become a cornfield or a wheatfield. If willows and maples grow along its edges then the marsh tends to become filled with trees and is changed into a woods.

But I have rambled far afield from these northern woods which prompted the wonder of my queries. The marsh and the mountains—they wait for further exploration. Today I am in a pine-hemlock forest. I see that some white birches have come in where an old tree went down some years ago, can understand the eventual change-over to what, a hundred years from now, may be a very different kind of forest. Sometimes the process of change is faster than this gradual displacement, not coming in here and there to develop an ultimately different appearance, but rather making a clean sweep. This is the hard way, the cruel way, the way which shows the orderly sequence of the return of the forest in perhaps the clearest manner. This is the way it is with fire.

Fires of the past might have burned for days, for weeks, until stopped by rain or by some part of the landscape which formed a natural firebreak. Then the stark, burned, charred skeletons of trees stood gaunt and lifeless. Dead deer, porcupines, partridges, squirrels, and bears might lie where they fell. The scavengers came in at once, hesitantly at first, venturing over the scarred and still smoking, blackened earth from which all the humus might have been consumed. Blowflies laid their eggs in carcasses, burying beetles tugged at bits of decaying flesh. They pulled away and buried it, with their eggs embedded in it—life to come from death. Crows and ravens as black as the charcoaled shards of pines came in to feast. Slowly, the signs of death vanished, though the dead trees remained.

For it takes a sustained fire to utterly burn to the ground a forest of trees which might be two to four hundred years old. The branches and needles go, but the great trunks remain upright.

Perhaps only the year after the big burn, perhaps that very year, the charred land turned green. Winds had brought flying seeds of aspen and birch. The silken fluff of the fireweed seeds blew in from somewhere, and they found a rooting. The next year that whole blackened area might be a garden of tall spires of the lavender-pink, four-petaled flowers of the fireweed. Beneath them could be growing the small young aspens and birches, and perhaps a few balsam firs.

Wild raspberry and blueberry bushes moved in after another year or so, sending their long roots out in colonial growth. A burned area was always the best place for the finest wild blueberries and the sweetest and most abundant red raspberries. The bushes found in the charred soil some special concentration of minerals which they needed for their richest growth.

In their small shade and in the shadow of the fireweeds, the seedlings of aspen, birch, and fir made a good start toward creating a new forest. By the time they were tall enough to make so much shade that further generations of fireweed could not grow, and when the blueberry bushes and the wild raspberries, now growing leggy, were not bearing as well as they did the bracken ferns had come in. They made a waist-high stand of horizontal, three-parted fronds, forming a lower story of greenery, like a secondary, miniature forest of their own beneath the now vigorous aspens and other quick-growing trees. In the greater shade made by the bracken, the wintergreen grew, often in large colonies, with the mosaic of bunchberry or dwarf cornel. Under the ferns there was concealment for the partridges which come to eat the berries, a hiding place for snowshoe hares and chipmunks and young foxes, a place for the ovenbird's nest on the ground, or for the partridge itself to make a nest for a dozen large buffy eggs. The bracken thickets concealed all paths and whatever walked on them or whatever lived close to the ground.

A few years later, except for the burned stubs of the largest trees, the horror and ruin of the fire had been largely forgotten and delicately concealed. Ten years later, the aspen woods had grown tall, letting in a flittering of sunshine through restless leaves which were hung in such a manner that they were seldom still. In the aspen leaf, the stem is round where it meets the twig, flat where it joins the blade. It is thus suspended for instant motion, even in no wind at all, and creates a continually fluctuating aspect of light and shade.

As years passed, the aspens became crowded out by a new generation of firs and pines, and young hemlocks were coming in with vigor. More and more, the last of the charred stubs fell down in storm and wind. The generations of aspen and birch leaves and the fallen needles of pine and fir had created humus over the once-denuded earth. Over logs, softening under the touch of snow and sun and the gnawing, chewing, probing, channeling of ants, wood-boring beetles, engraver beetles, and porcupines, and the devouring action of fungi and slime molds, the burned wood had sagged, collapsed, disintegrated, was blending with the earth.

Symbol of ruin, emblem of decay, the old stumps and logs nevertheless presented a picture of life and of certain endurance and continuity. They were all that remained of trees which had once grown and had had leaves and fruits and which, some time past, had been burned or cut or blown down in a wind. A vital part of the pattern of life in the woods, they had not wasted any part of themselves.

MUSHROOMS

In nature, destruction is sometimes construction, though it is often difficult to get the long-range view. Certain elements are locked in each creature and plant. At its death, the living elements are useless until they are unlocked and permitted once more to become part of the atmosphere, part of the earth, part of the lives of other creatures. Fungi of many sorts are among the first agents to begin this long process of constructive removal and a release of imprisoned elements into activity again. Mushroom spores come on the raw, cut surface of wood almost as soon as a tree is felled or broken or downed. The spores enter the wood, thrust out a silken white net-

Mushrooms

work of mycelium which is fragile yet powerful, possessing a sort of hunger which drains food from the cells of the wood. When the cells are depleted, they collapse in decay.

Indication of what is going on inside are the mushrooms bursting from the outside of stump or log—brackets, or velvet-stems, or sulphur mushrooms, Lenzites, Stereum, or Polyporous. Some are woody and may last for years; others are frail and vanish quickly. So selective are many fungi working on dead wood that some of them grow on and tear down only certain kinds of trees or dead wood—some on fir alone, some on pine and spruce, some only on the yellow birch, some on white birch, others only on red oak, some on other oaks, while still others live only on elm or willow. Slowly the old stump or log collapses, slumps lower, gently begins to merge its decaying wood with the earth, enriching it, returning its nutrients to the source from which it once drew them.

RENEWAL

And so the orderly pattern of renewal comes to the burned forest. As the balsams and spruces growing among the aspens finally crowd and shade them, the old aspens live out their lives, but few or finally no more young ones grow beneath them. The shade is now too great. The birches are also often superseded by the encroaching girth of the firs and by the white and red pines whose seedlings grow up among the other conifers in the shade they in turn provide. When there are hemlocks, finally, and yellow birches, a forest with deep shade and all its interlocking plant and animal life has come back.

It requires a long time for trees to become mature, yet the renewal of the forest after a fire may take only thirty years to produce one in which the signs of disaster are thoroughly hidden in the burgeoning growth and life of the present. But the big white pines in the forest of which I write have neither been burned nor cut. They have stood on land owned by a family who refused to permit loggers to come in for nearly a century. The trees were believed to be fully grown and huge at the beginning of that time, and are now no doubt between two hundred and fifty and three hundred years old. They are very tall, their pillars of trunks standing like Corinthian columns whose scrollwork of acanthus is replaced by the feathering of pine boughs at the top. Shade has long since caused a natural pruning of all the branches low down on the trunk.

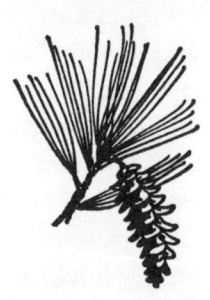

White Pine

As I came into the forest that day, the trees were so tall and their tops so dense that scarcely any breeze was felt down on the deer trail. The tops of the pines blew with a sound like surf on the rocks, and I could hear the sound washing in closer, closer, surging above my head as the boughs swished and shook. Then they grew quiet as the wind continued through the forest top and away from my hearing.

Thoreau mused:

"Sometimes I rambled in pine groves, standing like temples, or like fleets at sea, full-rigged, with wavy boughs, and rippling with light, so soft and green and shady that the Druids would have forsaken their oaks to worship in them. . . . Strange that so few ever come into the woods to see how the pine lives and grows and spires, lifting its ever-

THE CONIFEROUS FOREST

green arms to the light—to see its perfect success; but most are content to behold it in the shape of many broad boards brought to market, and deem *that* its true success. . . . These are petty and accidental uses; just as if a stronger race were to kill us in order to make buttons and flageolets of our bones; for everything may serve a lower as well as a higher use.

"Every creature is better alive than dead, men and moose and pine trees, and he who understands it aright will rather preserve its life than destroy it."

I could see that preserved life all about me as I walked the old trail—which unknown numbers of deer have also followed—and listened to the muted voices of the forest.

The hemlocks swept branches of small needles—peacock's-tails of branches—nearly to the ground. The floor beneath was so shaded, so cool, so damp, that the mosses had become very thick. They had upholstered every old rotting stump and log, had hidden all traces of any long-gone burn, gently covered the signs of outward decay while at the same time fostering it. For in holding the moisture in the decaying orange-brown wood by hiding its surface and thus preventing evaporation, the mosses aided in its further disintegration. To step unwisely upon one of these long, low ridges was to find my foot going disconcertingly down into a pulpy mass of wet, decaying wood. But the mosses hid all this nicely under their green mantle.

There were many kinds here, more varieties than I might find in a less damp and shaded and antiquated forest—knight's plume mosses, Thuidium, some so intricately branched that they were like elegant bronze-green ferns three inches long, some golden green, overlaid in a pattern to make a thick mat. There were beds of those miniature firs, the hair-cap moss, the little treelike moss called Climacium, and the hummocks of white moss, Leucobryum, like rounded pincushions. In the very wet places, where thin shamrocks of white wood sorrel grew, I found the large rosettes of rose moss, Rhodobryum. Porella liverworts were arranged in thick, inch-deep overlapping rows on tree trunks. Little prehistoric-looking Marchantia liverworts grew with the ground mosses. There were the curling thalluses of dog-lichens whose white undersides just showed, like coyly exhibited petticoat edges beneath somber gowns. It was a world of the mosses and lichens and liverworts, and of the soft banks of old man's beard lichens hanging in festoons like Spanish moss—there a pair of parula warblers had begun to build a nest.

Every log and stump and half-visible rock and stick seemed to be decorated with something alive and green which had set out to cover it totally. The populations of this northern forest, like that of the western rain forest itself, were inconceivable—not only the myriads of these tiny plants, and the amber snowflake flowers of bishop's cap, the ruby-lit clumps of the coral-root orchids, the low trailing beds of arbutus and partridgeberry, the miniature white violets an inch tall, but animal life as well.

Some of the animal life was microscopic, or nearly so, and occupied the lower parts of this damp, mossy, shadowed woods. It had its own part to play, just as the porcupine up in a yellow birch had a part, and the deer—a deer had been watching as I came into the woods, had stood quietly under the pines, observing without any particular alarm, then with a sudden whiffle of sound and a flick of a white tail had gone off into the thimbleberry thickets. The porcupine simply clung where it was, having plenty of time to wait, until I began to walk again, when it commenced chewing a twig with slow rasping sounds of long teeth. Somewhere just a little way off the deer no doubt was still watching.

WINTER WREN

I sat on a log which had some substance and would not immediately collapse under me, and listened. Far away in puddles, small frogs were singing—far in the distance, pinkletinks, the peepers awash in spring. Listen—somewhere, again the minors of the hermit thrush. Listen—a breathless and incredible burst of small music. This could not be real. I could not actually be hearing it, must surely imagine this intricate composition. A fairy music box, a thin, in-

Winter Wren

tricately-woven tinkling and cascading of high, silver-hewn notes—listen, the winter wren!

I could not see the bird. The song went on and on and on, as if the maker did not know how to stop. When it did halt, it seemed that I must still be hearing the notes, and then they poured forth all over again—just as elaborate, just as complex, just as high and as infinitely sweet, thin, and rapid, and with that quality of polished silver. I knew that if the song of a winter wren could be expressed in substance, the notes must be silvery and have wings on their staffs, and they must come tumbling out of somewhere in a froth-cloud, like one's breath on a frosty morning, only expressed in music.

On a slanting, broken-backed hemlock which had gone down in a wind yet had not quite broken through, but had left long, shattered red-brown splinters standing to the sky, I saw a diminutive bird. It was all brown, its short tail cocked at the proper wren angle but exaggerated so that it tilted quite over its back. It flounced and twitched and dallied along the broken wood, investigated a cranny, probed its beak quickly into a crevice of bark, and seemed to find something edible. The bird bobbed suddenly to the tip of a great splinter, tucked down its short tail and lifted its beak to the arching pines—and again the music box sounded, and all that shivering, tinkling silver poured forth again.

The winter wren's song is one of the incredible and fitting parts of the atmosphere of an old and mossy forest. The bird is found nesting here as well as in old cedar swamps. In summer it is almost always found only in these dark, remote places of the north. The winter wren is as much a part of the forest's character as the veery and the hermit thrush. While the veery usually prefers the hardwoods, the hermit thrush belongs in the coniferous places, and I could hear one singing now, as I had been hearing it all the way inland from the sand ridges, a distant, melancholy fluting. Both it and the wren possess a special character of mystery and of things not seen and of sounds not heard. For I wonder, after I have listened in awe to the cascading, high notes of the winter wren, just how many more notes I have not heard at all, and how much longer the song actually lasts after I have ceased to hear it.

Many birds no doubt sing songs we never hear at all—think what unknown arias the hummingbird might be uttering among the scarlet columbines! But the winter wren, fortunately for us who sometimes come into the depths of its old mossy forests where the hermit thrush is also singing, does let itself be heard, or at least in part. But I shall still wonder about the portions of the song which surely I never hear at all.

John Burroughs knew woods which must have been similar to these, for he too was acquainted with the thrush and the wren, and wrote about them in his "Bird and Bush":

> In the primal forest's hush,
> Listen! . . . the hermit thrush!
> Silver chords of purest sound
> Pealing through the depths profound;
> Tranquil rapture, unafraid
> In the fragrant morning shade.
> Purest sounds are farthest heard,
> Voice of man or song of bird;
> And the hermit's silver horn
> In dreaming night or dewy morn
> Is a serene, ethereal psalm,
> Devoutly gay, divinely calm—
> The soul of song, the breath of prayer,
> In melody beyond compare.

THE CONIFEROUS FOREST

And winter wren with thee abides—
A dapper bird that skulks and hides;
Pert his mien, his wondrous throat
Quivers and throbs with rapid note—
A lyric burst with power imbued
To thrill and shake the solitude.

THE CEDAR FOREST

Adjoining the pines and merging with them, yet apart, stood the old white cedars, the arbor vitae forest. They formed a buffer between the pines and the lake storms and winds, perhaps had been doing so for centuries, had grown here and had so protected the big forest that the wind only blew through its top. The cedars had taken the brunt of hard weather and gale winds and snows for so long that they must have been well braced for it. In enduring the twisting, wrenching force of wind, their trunks showed a spiraling grain; the furrows in the bark itself went up in a spiral, while the dead wood in those that had perished presented much the same violently twisted appearance as similar trees high in the Rocky Mountains. Their very grain, to the core, had been influenced by weather and mightily wrenched by strain.

Because they stood on a fairly shallow soil above bedrock, their roots had had to extend themselves laterally and could not go very deeply except in probing into deep crevices below ground. In storms, now and again, a cedar blows down and lies upended, roots in the air, or else has simply tilted and still lives because the rooting at a few points holds tight. The forest, because of this, in parts was like a great jackstraw game in which the dead, downed trees lay crisscrossed or were slanted at grotesque angles. Among fallen trees there were some very old ones from which all branches and roots had been weathered and worn off. These trunks lay supine, disintegrating, deeply mossy, and almost indistinguishable from the hummocky, needle-covered floor of the old forest.

Thinking that they looked something like long green graves, I could see the metaphor—they really were graves of fallen trees. No doubt the whole uneven contour of the forest floor had been caused by ancient generations of defunct trees which had finally merged with the earth, yet had left their contours visible under the moss.

On a log which still kept its identity, though beautifully upholstered with mosses and an elegant matting of dark green snowberry vines, I saw a row of young cedars, several seedling balsam firs, and a white pine. They were indeed in a row, although of obviously different ages. Two of the young balsams had reached the noble height of a foot; the pine, three inches high, had a single tuft of soft needles, and most of the cedars, with their lower scales still bristly, the upper ones oval and braided in appearance, were an inch to three inches in height. But the row-planting was strangely coincidental. They were arranged as if on purpose along the top of the fallen trunk, at the zenith of its curve. Evidently the seeds had fallen into the thick, damp moss, had easily germinated, had sent their roots into the acid, mineral-filled moisture of decayed wood, and had started to grow in a rooting medium which was perfect for coniferous seedlings. Eventually, if they survived, their roots would push down through the nourishment of the decayed wood into the earth at last.

Not until I saw the red squirrel perched cockily, foxy tail bent neatly back along his spine, furry haunches well braced as he sat upright, did I realize how the young conifers came to be planted as they were. Almost every mossy old log had its embryo forest.

The squirrel was busily shucking out the seeds from the small clusters of cedar cones. The remains of old balsam fir cones were littered about also, with a spruce cone or two. The scales were there, empty and dry; so also were a few seeds themselves. The squirrels had not always eaten everything. The minute weight of the seed portion pointed it down into the moss, the thin, winged vane standing upright—the seed thus was in the proper position for germination. It was the correct sprouting and growing medium, a situation brought about by the squirrel.

In their own way, the squirrels had seen to perpetuating the forests of the north. Just as the fox and gray squirrels farther south bury walnuts and acorns for future reference and then never come back to dig them all up, and new trees sprout and grow, so the bright-eyed, sassy little red squirrels of the north have seen to the continuation of the forests which mean their own livelihood and their own perpetuation. Not knowingly, of course. The squirrel or jay planting an acorn and covering it up, and the red squirrel shucking seeds from cones, are simply taking care of their hunger, either for the future or of the moment. If some of the provender isn't eaten and manages to sprout, it is none of their knowing or their conscious doing. But it is nature's doing, and the means are served in many and devious methods of seed dispersal.

This is surely one of the neatest methods of all, however—to equip cones with seeds which are relished by squirrels, then to give the squirrel the sort of quirk which insists that he take his food to a point of vantage somewhere, a log or stump, where he naturally sits upon the highest elevation and proceeds to get out the seeds. It is provided also that some of the seeds should slip from the animal's grasp and ken; though winged, they are heavy at one end so that they naturally tip downward and slide between the plants of moss. The likelihood of the seeds' germinating on the ground itself is far less than if they lie protected in moss where the moisture is held, the nutrient supply unlimited, and the chance of being discovered by chipmunk, mouse, or partridge the less. The seed has thus been put exactly where it will grow best and survive, and so the forest itself survives.

Aware now of the significance of the low green mounds, I was suddenly seeing them everywhere as long narrow tree nurseries. Almost every one of them was outfitted with an assortment of baby trees, some of them sizeable now, their original sprouting place all but lost as the growing roots pushed it aside and engulfed it.

Beneath the cedars, with their aromatic fans of scale leaves overlaid upon the twigs, the shade was very dark indeed. The light meter was of little help in locating sunshine for photographs other than time exposures or flash pictures. This forest, besides, was not easy to walk through, except along the deer trail, for the cedars had great numbers of dead lower branches which had all remained on the tree, slanting downward in a bristling barricade of long sharp spines.

There were damp, boggy hollows in the middle of the woods where algae and moss grew thick and noxious, like something in a dinosaur's swamp. But the slopes were sparkling with the white flowers of the goldthread, in whose crystal-white petals and glossy green, three-parted leaves the scant light of the forest seemed caught. The roots, I knew, were like thin gold wires, very bitter and medicinal, used in treating throat ailments in pioneer times. The plants, small, low, and compact, are one of the carpet plants of the Boreal Zone. Goldthread follows the spruce and cedar forests all the way to the edge of trees in the subarctic.

The goldthread's external simplicity—only a tiny white flower—is belied by its botanical complexity. What appear to be petals are sepals, five to seven of them, in the undecided counting of the Ranunculus family. Around the petal-like sepals stand numerous tiny, glistening white clubs, evidently long-modified petals themselves which have become nectaries with a potent lure for certain extremely minute fungus gnats and sometimes tiny beetles. There are often two dozen white stamens tipped with yellow anthers, and a cluster of pistils or carpels, three to seven of them—all these things arranged within the compass of the one small flower which is seldom more than half an inch wide.

It was a woman who discovered the little goldthread—a woman

Goldthread

who possibly felt an affinity for bogs and the chill northern forests, for she could have found it nowhere else. Miss Jane Colden collected it in upper New England in 1758. It should more appropriately have been named in her honor—"Coldenella," perhaps. It was instead named *Coptis trifolia*, the word *coptis* meaning cut, because of the three-parted leaves. Perhaps there was an aversion to women botanists at that time.

THE CEDAR SWAMP

Where the cedars moved down a slope to a boggy area, and then stayed in these lower reaches to become a cedar swamp, I found the greatest concentration of mosses and other upholstering. Everything was covered thickly, roots and hummocks and fallen trees, greenery creeping up trunks themselves, so that no inch of earth or mud or water showed among the old trees. They stood with their roots in a black, acid water and muck, on a peat bottom of unknown age. They curved and arched over and through the moss and into the water, in an almost reptilian manner, leaving hollows between where it was easy for one to slip and find a foot caught beneath solid wood. In the green shade grew more of the little goldthread flowers, and the pure white, sparkling stars of the three-leaved Solomon's seal, and an interlacing of twinflower vines with a myriad of buds just showing pink.

A frog leaped in a long green slither from a mossy root into a black pool on which the oil stain of dead diatoms seemed ancient in time. The winter wren sang in the distance. No breeze stirred the draperies of Usnea lichens hanging from slanting trees. A pink moccasin flower was poised on a sphagnum hump among the cedar roots. At first there was only this one orchid—sudden, startling, and magnificent—and then there were others, and others, until I stood in the realm of the pink moccasin flowers.

With them here and there, and in farther places where I saw that a little more light came in and set golden-green sunshine on the moss, the white-furred crosiers of cinnamon and interrupted ferns were just now uncoiling and beginning to stand tall. Out in the open wet meadows the ferns had been up and tall long before this, but in the chill shadows of the swamp they were always very late. Now they lifted their tight, coiled fronds in immense dignity, the curled pinnae opening inch by inch as the stalks grew taller. Fruiting fronds appeared to be wands covered as with an orange-cinnamon fish roe—the granular massing of the brightly colored spores set a brilliant splash of color under the cedars and on the green world of the mossy underpinning. Some of the fruiting stalks were knee-high, bending over a little at the tip.

It was time to turn back. Where the cedar swamp opened into more light, there were dwarf birches five feet tall. On the tundra around Hudson Bay and northward, they might be less than a foot. There also were alder bushes in the swamp. When I see tangles of alder, I know it is time for me to turn back.

Of all the disagreeable, wearisome, maddening, exhausting areas in the northern wild, the alder thickets are, in my opinion, by far the worst. They are not tall enough to be trees so that I can walk beneath them without ducking and struggling to get between their sprangling branches which spring, gnarly and muscular, from the root bases. They are not low enough for me to push through or to see above. After having been in them more than once, and having regretted the experience every time, having come out fly-bitten and mosquito-tormented, with hair torn and skin scratched, wet to the knees and disgusted, I avoid alder thickets whenever possible. Still, the alder is beautiful in early spring. The purple-brown catkins which have stayed all winter on the twigs, along with the neat little black cones, lengthen in very early spring and cast pollen into the air. The newly forming cones are green all summer, ripening and turning black by winter. But I prefer to look at alders from their outskirts, not from their midst.

It was more comfortable to walk in the big quiet forest with its cool green light and misty lavender distances, to come back to the pines where the deer watched and where the porcupine again left off chewing to freeze to even greater immobility until I went on, and where a ruffed grouse was drumming somewhere far off. The winter wren created an enchanted music which was a suitable background and part of the atmosphere of the old coniferous forest.

The pines were still. The wren was quiet. The thrush had stopped singing, and warblers in the plumy treetops were silent. There was only the distant, incessant piping of the little frogs, and the sound of chopping as a woodpecker tackled a tree. The myriad breathing and living and dying and disintegrating and rebirth of the forest were all about me. Without man's tampering, the forest would continue indefinitely with its intricate changes, its constant renewal, and its tearing down and rebuilding in the long and patient pattern of the years. For the forest is a community, a great multiple-limbed entity. It is not one tree or one bird or one moss bank. It is that whole interlocking complex of many creatures all living together, dependent upon each other's success as individuals for their own success, their lives and deaths mingling and interchanging wonderfully in a great unit which is the forest.

CHAPTER EIGHT

THE DECIDUOUS WOODS

COOL and green and mysterious in the half-light of dawn, the deciduous woods stood very still and without any motion of leaf or bird or butterfly. It was too late for the night creatures still to be out foraging—except for the pair of skunks down in the dew-soaked meadow, grubbing about with claws and noses. The raccoons had returned from their prowling and had climbed into their bed-trees. The barred owl had gone back to the hemlock where he liked to spend the day. The friskers and foragers who had been active in the past night's moonlight were out of sight.

It was too early for the daytime creatures to have stirred in the spring chill. Not even the migrant warblers, which had been pouring into the treetops for several days and which surely had not all gone on in the night, were evidently awake. A robin had sung before daylight; I had heard the guttural tweeting of purple martins somewhere in the dark; a restless tootling came from the gulls sitting out on the bay where they had spent the night. Blue jays had begun their bugling as soon as a little light had come to the lake and had caught highlights in the dew hanging on leaves at the fringe of the forest. Few birds would be active until the sun finally rose and warmed the upper branches.

Early morning is always somewhat like the dawn of creation itself. There is a freshness, a newness, as if yesterday had never been and tomorrow would be anticlimactic. There is only now, today, this day, this place, the first day when the woods stand completed, with dew on all the white trilliums, the violets still indistinct in the shadows, and yellow bellwort pendants half concealed under drooping blue-green leaves and each leaf and petal tipped with moisture.

It is May in the woods. It is as springtime has come into many woods across the country, with many variations of the springtime pattern, yet most of them expressing the same basic truths in much the same theme: the carrying over of life from one year to the next in terms of the blossoming, the singing, the leafing, the growing, and the reproducing which are the assurances that life continues through still another season. These woods are different with every spring and with every day. Yet always some of that same basic pattern of growth follows through, piece by piece, part by part, in orderly fashion, like a jigsaw puzzle which is carefully put back together again with each returning bird and each emerging flower to help fill the pattern.

It starts with the first thaw and the first new catkin, with the first hepatica and the first robin. Yet although the arrangement may be the same, it is always different, too; and there is never enough time to see it all before the pattern changes again. I never really get to see the finished picture, for when this spring design is completed with all its parts in place, it is not, after all, a picture of spring, but of summer. Spring is noteworthy for its character of incompletion, of its anticipation of what tomorrow will bring, for its feeling of assurance which comes as each bird returns on time and each flower opens and each new leaf unfurls in its traditional manner, each kind in its own way. It is a period of filling in, of adding to, of arriving and departing; it is wonderfully exciting and ever new.

These woods are old, and even during the newness and transience of spring, they presented a finished look. The tall beeches and maples, the lower story of the younger beeches, leatherwood, viburnum shrubs, and the witch hazel, the ground cover of ferns and spring flowers, the multitudes of young maple seedlings, the comfortable carpeting of damp old leaves and mushrooms, and the soft, moisture-holding earth under all—all these formed the picture I saw on a morning in May.

Yet neither these woods nor any others ever came here fully grown and filled with life. They all had had to start with the bare earth and add, subtract, and multiply in innumerable changes and successions. The comforting thing about a destroyed woodland is that, like the burned forest, it will not stay ruined. These particular woods proved it. They had suffered what might seem to have been almost endless and insurmountable disasters, yet they had continued in their patient patterns of orderly regrowth, over and over and over again for thousands of years.

Whatever kinds of woods were here at the time of the Ice Age, they were all swept away and the whole area cleared off down to the bedrock, as clean as if with a steam shovel. Then, with the going of the ice, the return of vegetation took place, and with it the slow development of leaf mold.

Very likely the plants were not the same sorts which had been here before the ice, nor which are here now. No doubt in the cold, almost sterile sand and gravel and transported clays which had been dumped by the glacier on top of the limestone, only the low heaths, some of the carpet plants, could dwell. Then came

THE DECIDUOUS WOODS

spruces and firs, then pines and hemlocks of the big primeval forest.

It was never left in peace, unassaulted and undamaged; and even before white men came here, there were fires. Their scars lie deep within some of the arbor vitae trees clinging, gnarled and huge and incredibly durable, on the rim of the cliffs. These trees have been here for hundreds of years, outlasting the old forest, the lumbering, and the fires, and have built and maintained a windbreak, a shield against lake storms, for the woods which have developed over and over again behind them. In so doing, the arbor vitae here have a very different aspect from that of their kin in the old cedar forest or out in the shelter they build behind the first ridge. On the cliffs, the trees are twisted in a furious grip in and among the rocks, in maintaining their impervious hold. Ice may form on the rocks and the beach below, may cover cliffs and trees when winds blow stormwaters upward. The ice-glazed trees stand with a blinding glitter in the winter sunshine. Their woody roots are like great fists clutching the cliffs, while others are like stout props which grope down through fissures in the limestone to reach the beach level almost seventy feet below, or descend even deeper to reach water.

The first big lumbering took out the big pines which grew behind the arbor vitae wall. The forest promptly filled in the gaps; then a second cutting took out most of the remaining pines and the second-growth trees as well, leaving only young ones and a few small hemlocks which weren't worth anything commercially. For a time there must have been many aspens in the opening brought about by the cutting, and beneath their lightly shuttered shade the usual succession of balsams and birches and pines must have been growing. But as hardwoods also came in abundantly, they finally supplanted most of the conifers, so that the renewed forest became a beech-maple stand instead.

When again the lumbering operations moved in, the trees in this punished place were considered worth nothing more than firewood, so they were cut off—the big maples and beeches—and taken by sailing ship down the coast to feed the wood-stove economy of

Milwaukee and Chicago. And once again the process of reseeding and orderly successions rebuilt the forest around the nucleus of young trees which had not been large enough to be cut, even for kindling wood. The area became a mixed woods with a few pines, hemlocks, balsams, and white spruces here and there to tell of its past affiliations, and with aspens around the sunny edges, the arbor vitae still holding firm on the cliffs.

As the woods were rebuilt, there was shade once more, there were ferns and deep-woods plants. Yet, because mainly deciduous trees grew here, there was enough spring openness before the leaves came out to foster trilliums and lady's-slippers, anemones, bloodroot, hepaticas, clintonias, yellow adder's-tongues, and the beautiful, northern, long-spurred violets. One more fire came through in the early part of this century. It spread unchecked from a careless blaze in a haystack half a mile or so away, and damage was done around the bases of the beeches and a scarring left on many of the birches and aspens.

In the past thirty years there have been neither fires nor cutting. One hundred and thirty-five acres of forest are accented by two open meadows to mark where a pioneer farmer had tried to carve a farm out of woods set on stony soil lying too close to the bedrock to be very suitable for crops.

The meadows add significance to the meaning of the forest. They present a pattern of sunshine on grass and of open sky with moving clouds, as a contrast to the drama and shadows of the woods. The trees continually encroach on the meadows, and one is even now being determinedly taken over by ranks of aspens followed by firs and maples, and some white pines. But the lower meadow remains open. It is bordered with a tall margin of panicled dogwood, with large-toothed aspens standing behind it, and the deeper forest beyond their windbreak and shelter.

The woods have been protected from disaster for so long that the trees have grown larger and their shade broader in the ensuing years. The wild flowers, protected from the menaces of grazing, burning, picking, and lumbering have multiplied as they perhaps had not had a chance to do since before the big cutting. Now thousands of great white trilliums, hundreds of yellow lady's-slippers and several other kinds of orchids, drifts of violets and wood anemones, dwarf ginseng, corydalis, yellow adder's-tongues, hepaticas, bloodroot, wild sarsaparilla, wild leek, white baneberry, columbine, and clintonia are the smiling face of the natural springtime woods as I come into these quiet, cool haunts on a morning in May.

The timeless renewal of the wild is proved by the woods. They conceal the tragedies of the past, yet the scars are still there, only decently hidden, blending with the living landscape—ancient stumps, charred trunks, an old wall of field stone laid up with back-breaking work by the pioneer farmer and his sons. Marks of the Ice Age are here—pockets of gravel—and the ancient Silurian seas which formed the limestone have left their mark in the stone wall itself, in the whole cliff-underpinning of the woods, and in the occasional fossil which appears in the path.

THE TREES

Primarily, of course, the whole source and secret of any woods must depend upon the trees, and you must have successful trees to have a comfortable and enduring forest. Yet, to any creature which uses it or knows it, a tree has a different evaluation of success—not knowingly, of course, but the instinctive evaluation is there. To the caterpillar of the Polyphemus moth, the birch was eminently useful because it provided in ample quantity the leaf-food required by the larva to attain its metamorphosis into a moth. The tree also supplied the wherewithal for a cocoon's support, and was a place to which to cling when the moth struggled forth.

To the luna moth, the birch also had meaning. There was a lovely green luna holding quietly to a shoot beneath a birch that morning, a moth with lettuce-colored wings and a white-furred

Birch (LEFT)
Quaking Aspen (RIGHT)

body marked with violet. The cocoon had been made among the birch leaves; but instead of fastening the structure with waterproof silk to the pendant twig as the Polyphemus had done, the luna rolled its cocoon in a leaf. Then when the leaf fell off in autumn, so did the cocoon; and it lay beneath the snow all winter. The moth emerged in May. Both to the green luna and the fawn-colored Polyphemus, the birch had been a success.

The wood pewee, one of the flycatchers, found the tree's best use was in providing a horizontal branch on which a neatly constructed, lichen-ornamented nest could be built with the assurance of ample support. By using binoculars, I could locate an old nest on a solid branch, and there would no doubt soon be another for this year's brood of pewees. The tree also provided a convenient dead branch or two which made an opening in the forest greenery and served as a high perch for the pewee, so that it might see passing insects and dart out to snatch them.

The robin-sized, noisy, crested flycatcher would also use the dead branches for the same purpose, but would take a hole in a tree for a nest. It might be an abandoned woodpecker hole, for these serve many uses after the original owners have built new ones.

To the woodpecker, the tree is not only a place in which to chisel a cavity for a nest or a winter bed, but a medium into which to sink its powerful beak in rapid-fire blows, sending chips flying, as the bird goes after a wood-boring grub. A small downy woodpecker just then was attacking a dead limb, the staccato hammering resounding through the morning woods. A heavy thumping in the distance told me a big pileated woodpecker was at work, no doubt

THE DECIDUOUS WOODS

hewing out big chips as the bird sought food deep inside the tree.

In there live the juicy brown carpenter ants which make tunnels in the wood. To the ants the tree is successful when it is dead and easiest to gnaw, wood-grain by wood-grain, in making their extensive galleries and tunnels. The woodpecker finds the tree successful because it harbors food. But both as a habitation and foraging ground for birds and insects, the success ends when the woodpecker has destroyed the ant colony, or when bears have broken open the trunk for the same purpose.

To the chickadee hunting a nest cavity in April, the tree is now desirable because the woodpecker has left an unoccupied hole which is just right for chickadees, as it was also just suited to the crested flycatcher. Into the pileated woodpecker's large excavation the wood duck may thrust her head and then slip inside to make a nest. A screech owl may take over the hole. A raccoon may bed down in some rotted hollow which may have begun many years ago as a woodpecker's digging in the realm of the now long-gone ants. For the uses of many creatures the tree is a success—to molds and mosses, to fungi and ferns, to birds and insects and mammals.

But the tree itself, unaided by other creatures or things, in its own perfection of growth—in simply being a tree—is a success. It has sprung from one small seed in whose carefully arranged cells the processes of growth and the pattern of leaves, flowers, fruit, wood cells, twigs, and buds were all preplanned and ready to proceed as soon as the first root went into the ground and the first leaves headed toward the light. This was success in itself, this in-

Sugar maple (LEFT)
Beech (RIGHT)

tuitive direction-finding of root and shoot going in opposite directions. For the work of the tree, just in being a tree, is mightily complex, and begins immediately after the seed sprouts. A tree must draw up water and minerals from the soil by means of the powerful pull of roots and root-hairs, must conduct fluids often a hundred feet or more up the pipeline system of xylem tubes to the outermost reach of the highest twigs and the farthest leaves. The leaves are manufacturing plant food by means of chlorophyll, sunlight, raw materials, and carbon dioxide, and the water brought up from the ground is vital.

For the leaves give off water as well as take it in; they create invisible fountains of vapor from every tree. They must also change starches into soluble sugars, transport them in solution down the food pipeline, the phloem tubes, to be stored or used immediately. The tree builds new cambium tissue under the bark each year, converts old cambium into heartwood, extends each twig an inch to three feet, depending upon the species, in a few weeks of rapid growth in spring. All these things and a good many more are parts of the magnificent fulfillment of the tree. So completely self-contained is it, in its long-term plan of growth, that only the oldest part of the cambium layer, made no more than several years ago, is perhaps all that is actively alive in the deciduous tree from one year to the next—only that thin, vital, life-layer and the buds which carry the cell structure and leaf plan are alive from autumn to spring.

To the buds are entrusted the future of the tree, and in them lies the traditional pattern of the species. It will be spurred to growth by energy from last summer's sunshine. All day long the tree's leaves absorb energy and store it as sugars in the wood. When I burn a log for heat or light, I am using the energy which was put there by leaves growing years ago, and in burning it I liberate the heat by means of oxidation of the carbon and hydrogen atoms. Even before the wood is burned to release heat, some is given off by the living tree. The trunk of course does not feel warm to the

THE DECIDUOUS WOODS

touch, but there is a palpable difference in temperature in the winter woods as compared with that in the open. The temperature in a hardwood forest in midsummer may be ten degrees lower by day, because of shade from the leaves and their cooling effect of transpired vapor, and ten degrees higher at night because of that retained heat.

During spring growth the energy in the sap generates heat from the intensified oxidation, just as the animal body grows warmer in exertion. Buds expand, and leaves grow in their own heat, as the skunk cabbage in the marsh is enabled to push up through frozen muck and snow, and to blossom long before other flowers. The skunk cabbage, together with many other spring plants, and the growing buds and leaves, actually runs a temperature which may be many degrees higher than its surroundings.

With this spurt of inner warmth in early spring, the deciduous woods are enabled to come quickly into bloom. It is the one opportunity in the whole year when there are both enough light and moisture, as well as a gentle warmth—at least above thirty-five degrees F. for flowers to blossom in the woods. Only now they may make leaves and food, and set their seeds, and it is all to be done in a great hurry before tree-leaves shut out the sunshine. Thus, the plants from all the prearranged buds on roots and in bulbs must shoot up quickly. Most are pushed and expanded and stiffened by water pressure and turgor rather than by the cellulose which strengthens and holds up the leaves and stems of later plants. There is not enough time in spring for a plant to produce very much fiber or very many leaves, or much length of stalk. But water is usually plentiful and as long as plant cells are filled tightly with it, the leaves and stems stand firmly upright. Deprived of the water supply, as when they are picked, or when the sun is unseasonably warm for spring, or when the wind is strong and drying, they quickly wilt. Those early flowers are opportunists. They have chosen the one time in the year when they can have what they require for life and growth and the chance to make seeds.

JOURNEYS IN GREEN PLACES

THE ROOTS OF SPRING

Those roots of this spring, which make all this fast growth possible, were prepared last year. The assurance of what I found on a May morning was all ready last summer, ready for this very morning, then put away in cold storage to be brought out when the time was right and the need for growth was immediate and quick. Though they have been ready since last summer and autumn, they would not, with but few exceptions, appear too early. Their timing and chemistry are such that they require a resting period and, preferably, in northern species, a period of freezing. In some, the latter requirement is essential. Grown in more southern climates,

Bloodroot

these cold-inured plants usually become ineffectual, lose strength, and, in a year or so, no longer bloom. Freezing, or at least cold weather, apparently is needed to trigger the change of starches to sugars, and of sugars to flooding the growth mechanism with energy.

Sometimes only a short period of cold will be enough to effect the great change. Then when the time signal rings in the individual plant, it will bloom as quickly as it can get out of the ground. This accounts for all those gratifyingly hasty hyacinths, crocuses, daffodils, and tulips in the garden, and the spring beauties, bloodroot, hepaticas, marsh marigolds, trout lilies, and anemones which are a delight to find in the morning of the year.

This contrast of the springtime with the rigors of the deep

cold and snow is one of the rewards for living in the northern half of America. This is the fulfillment of the promises made last spring, the maturing of growth made last summer, the result of events which took place last fall. They are the reward for the winter which we and they have just survived.

The early spring flowers in this fragrant May woodland were also one of the results of the Ice Age. In those years of very long winters and very short summers, there was not always enough time for a plant to make leaves, develop to the point of producing flowers, and ripen its seeds before the snows again were upon it. Advance preparation was the answer.

TROUT LILY OR ADDER'S-TONGUE

When the trout lily or adder's-tongue grows suddenly in April or early May, it quickly puts forth grown leaves and flower stem.

Trout lily

There still were a few butter-yellow adder's-tongues in bloom that day when I walked in those woods. But most of them had already made their seeds in three-sided, pale-green pods, while the spotted, pale, silvery-green leaves were looking spent and yellowed as their work neared its end. The adder's-tongue—which I really prefer to call trout lily, because it is a lily, and a lovely one indeed— puts up a three- or four-inch stem bearing a single bent bud standing between the pair of leaves. The bud is a soft yellow shaded with violet; and when the flower opens and curls back its petals like a miniature Easter lily, this violet color remains on the backs of the three sepals. The six parts of the blossom are yellow, and only that purplish tinge on the three outer parts differentiate them from the petals themselves. Six stamens and a curving pistil with a three-parted stigma thrust from the lily bell.

East of the Rockies, there are two trout lilies or adder's-tongues, this yellow one of the east and north, and the white trout lily of the middle west. In the western mountains there are pink and lavender kinds, and bright-yellow ones—snow lilies at the rim of melting glaciers.

Although the trout lily's annual work is nearly finished for the year when many other kinds of spring flowers are just coming up and others are just opening, it may have waited seven years for this day. For it is required of every flowering plant to make a certain number of leaves before it is mature enough to bloom. The number varies with each species. Some may take all summer to make enough leaves—the goldenrods and asters and sunflowers, for instance. Others do it more rapidly and are able to bloom in late May, June, or early July.

Because the trout lilies and many more of those early-blooming flowers, use the food which their required leaves made last year, they do not now need to wait. There is instead a great urgency to carry on their life processes while enough light remains in the forest. And that energy which is replenished once more in root or bulb—when this season's rapid growth is finished, matured, and ended—remains through this summer and autumn, and winter. Energy simply waits in the roots for the right moment—for the coming of the thaw, the correct number of light hours in a day, and moisture to spur growth—to trigger plants into sudden activity again.

To fulfill the destiny of one trout lily, the plant needs a pair of slender, silvery, mottled leaves, a bulb with a few white roots, and one stem bearing one blossom—just two leaves and one flower for the complete plant above ground. In the extensive beds of trout lilies, however, I always find hundreds of one-leafed plants which

THE DECIDUOUS WOODS

do not bloom. These are not old enough as plants to produce flowers, have not yet made enough leaves, for the trout lily must be five to seven years old before it attains that maturity and blooms for the first time. Year after year the tiny bulb growing from a seed pushes deeper into the earth, and each spring it sends up one slender leaf. Then, in the year when the plant's timing mechanism decrees that it is old enough, two leaves come up; and there is at last that one small, handsome lily flower growing between them.

By the time leaves have expanded on the trees and shade has changed the living conditions on the floor of the forest, the trout lily and others which come very early have accomplished their growth. They have filled the one niche given to them in the crowded world of the forest, when there is sun enough to give them food and life.

BIRCHES

The open spring woods that day were filled with blossoms and sunshine as the light grew and the sun came flooding in. The birch grove shone with immaculate boles picked out in the light and topped only lightly as yet with a feathering of golden-green new leaves. When I had walked here in the moonlight the night before, there had been little real darkness. The birches had seemed to absorb the moonlight and to shine with an illumination of their own.

White things had stood out plainly, even the white stripe on the skunk's tail. In great dignity, the nodding plume had gone ahead of me on the trail, only the white markings visible. An ovenbird had awakened in the brilliance and uttered a startling cascade of notes which had not been at all like its daytime song—until the bird reached the ecstatic end and then signed it with the characteristic "teacher-teacher-*teacher!*" Although I could not see the bird in the darkness and light, its voice for a few moments seemed to fill the woods.

The spring woods under the moon were a place of mystery and wonder, with the spotlighting picking out not only the tall white candles of the birches but every three-parted flower of hundreds of white trilliums growing there, and every fluff of the dwarf ginseng and Canada mayflower, every pale violet and wood anemone. New ferns, new flowers, new leaves—they all presented a compounded fabric and perfume both in moonlight and in sunshine. They were all a part of the birch woods in springtime.

Birches were one of the commonest trees during glacial times. They were pushed south only because the great ice stood on top of their preferred haunts, only moved beyond the actual rim of the ice itself, then readily came back in a wave of white to replant the newly thawed areas. Birches have always been the newcomers in northern places. The wind blows their thin, gauze-winged little seeds off into burned uplands or into broad, empty acreages which need populating. There, with all the light they need, they thrive in impoverished growing conditions, long winters, and short summers.

The paper birch and its kin are unique trees, truly trees of the north. They are fitted to withstand the ultraviolet rays of winter sunshine cast at them from sky and snow, equipped to endure extreme cold, and armored against excessive drying and the work of winds. Yet they decorate the edge of a gentle, blue-water lake or ornament a glacial hill, the edge of a tundra, or a stony pasture with equal grace and facility. They show no indication, besides, of having been harmed or hampered by the coming of man across the landscape. The birches have, in fact, been benefited.

A good many trees may have grown fewer in numbers since man came, but the birches of the north have evidently increased. Their very nature as pioneers has saved them and has caused them to multiply, so that there are more today, ecologists believe, than there ever were in primitive times—more birches, but perhaps at the expense of the great vanished stands of pine and maple and beech which were destroyed in the great cutting, clearing, and burning.

As a tree of the Ice Age, the paper birch was unable to dwell

THE DECIDUOUS WOODS

comfortably for very long in the new postglacial heat and dryness which came into much of the middle west and south where the birch had been pushed during the time of the great expansion of the ice. The tree moved back north at once, for everything about it was specialized for extremes of northern temperament. In its very fibers, from root to twig-tip, it bore a certain quality of resilience which let the tree submit to strong winds, or to bend almost double in a white arc when an ice storm or heavy snow weighted its top and the birch bent over to touch the ground. Many trees break under such a strain. The birches simply go with the times, bow over, and, when the pressure is removed, the difficulty ended, spring erect. Some never quite stand up perfectly straight again, a mark to show that, for birches, bowing to fate is better for survival than breaking and perishing.

Aiding that resilience, the birch bears an extraordinary covering which is many-ply, laminated, waterproof, insulated, protecting the vital sapwood lying inside. The unique white bark is a prime asset in making great flexibility possible. A tree with a heavy, vertically-furrowed bark would never be able to bend so easily, for an armor-plating would crack and be ruined. But Betula, the birch, is wrapped in its many thin, pliable, papery layers of an arboreal plastic—surely almost as durable and versatile as any manmade pliofilms and polystyrenes of devious molecular construction.

This white substance stretches with the growth of the tree and does not split vertically as most tree bark does, although there may be many tiny, thin, horizontal splits or lenticles in the outer covering and young twigs, as in cherry bark. Wherever there was a branch, a triangular black scar remains. This specialized tree-skin is white because its cells are empty. They are like innumerable little mirrors, not filled with tannin or other substances to darken them, so that both sunlight and moonlight reflect from the minute, empty air spaces, as they do from snow, or gull feathers, or from the petals of the white water lily.

Beneath the white bark lies a corky, orange-brown layer of

insulation containing an antifreeze solution of volatile oils, sugars, and tannin, and beneath this is more of the colorful, tannin-filled, inner layer lying upon the living wood, the cambium or sapwood. The birch carries a great amount of cold protection both inside and out. In spite of its illusion of delicacy and fragility—of the naked white nymph shivering in forty degrees-F.-below-zero cold on a wind-swept northern hillside—the birch seems to have no difficulty in withstanding any amount of northern punishment. Southern kindness seems to be much more likely to destroy it.

It is the volatile oils in birch bark which cause that lively snapping and quick ignition when it is used as tinder to start a fire. Birch bark is the perfect fire-starter, obviously for the benefit of people living or camping in the north woods, for it is waterproof, and thus is not soaked in a prolonged rain. A natural paper which is ready for use—dry, oiled, thin enough to ignite at a spark—it is an excellent material for a quick fire.

Birds use birch bark too, but for a very different reason. The vireos which nest in the north woods carefully pull tissue-thin curls of white bark and interweave them into the fabric of a firm little basket-nest which may be securely suspended in a crotch of a twig, or even down in a hazel tangle or other low growth at the edge of the woods, a favorite location for a red-eyed vireo. The birch bark is so well integrated with the fabric of the nest that it *is* the nest, a clean, dry, strong, antiseptic white substance to hold eggs and young birds. It will last for years as a charming work of avian art; yet, sturdy and enduring though the nest is, the vireos nevertheless use it only once.

Perhaps, however, a wood mouse finds a low-lying vireo nest or the nest of another bird, and takes it over for a winter bed. The mouse may sometimes gather birch curls to use as a stuffing in the old nest, or to fill a tree cavity. There is nothing else quite like this special substance for the nest-builders and the bed-fillers of the north.

It lasts longer than the tree, for even after the birch is dead,

THE DECIDUOUS WOODS

the bark continues to encase the wood as it did in life. The inner wood may deteriorate, crumble, and disappear long before the bark will. Some say that it never decays, although this has certainly been far from proved. But the birch-bark casing, obviously lasting a good deal longer than the tree itself, is easily cut by a woodpecker. Through the bark, the birch Polyporous mushroom pushes like a forming blob of solid bubble gum. By the time the rotted bole is decorated with many of the expanded bracket mushrooms, all of them connected inside the dead wood by mycelium which absorbs the substance of the fiber, the whole thing weakens so much that it eventually topples. Yet, stretched on the ground, the tree's remains are still wrapped in the impermeable bark which covers the whole decaying, friable, wet mass.

When the interior has finally decayed away, the bark casing, like an empty stocking or an old paper bag, may lie collapsed on the floor of the woods. It may be pocked with sapsucker punctuations, cut into square holes by the hairy woodpecker, marked with round holes made by the downy woodpecker, and split by the protruding mushrooms. But it is still identifiable as birch bark, that long-enduring fabric of the north.

It had many uses by early peoples, who found it a water proof, lightweight material for building a canoe strong enough to carry three thousand pounds of weight in baggage and men, or a slim, light, swift canoe for one passenger. Birch canoes carried explorers to the Arctic and down the Mississippi. The bark was used by Indians for making utensils, buckets to catch dripping maple sap in the sugar bush in spring, baskets, pots, and cases. Slabs of bark made waterproof roofs for lodges, made raincoats and leggings. It became an early writing paper and wrapping paper, a natural parchment of infinite uses—that white parchment which was created by nature to suit the needs of the northern climate, and of the birch tree itself.

Its unique, chalky, shining white bark is its signature, and whenever it appears on a landscape, I know with a lifting of the heart and a mounting feeling of anticipation that I am going north—

north—north—have already neared my destination because there are birch trees once more in sight. When I reach the place where the white birches stand everywhere, I know that I also will find quaking aspens, white pines, balsam firs, tamaracks and swamp spruces, that I will find the plants of the cool Canadian carpet and the flavor of wintergreen. A single signature—a slender, indomitable white tree on the landscape.

When I came back to the woods in June, it was to a different place from the one I had known in spring. All the openness was gone, the flowers were gone, the sunlight was gone. A walk in the birch woods by moonlight was still a bright-patchy experience,

Trillium

but the birches were now all in leaf so that very little light flooded through. Leaves also shut out the sunlight, waylaid it up high in the canopy of the woods where the vireo sang in the heat. The vegetation of the forest floor, to compensate for this lack of light, seemed to be composed of leaves which were all very broad and very thin. They were built to take advantage of what little sunlight they could snare.

The birch woods lay at the edge of the deeper hardwood forest of beech, maple, basswood, and ironwood, and merged with it. The older climax forest where these trees grew was tremendously more shadowy in summer than even the birch woods, which had at least a degree of openness through which light passed.

In June, although the spring flowers were all gone, the leaves of some remained, and here and there I came upon a left-over

THE DECIDUOUS WOODS

columbine which the hummingbirds still visited. By midsummer only the leaves of hepatica and trillium and a few others marked where the hordes of spring flowers had been. There were now very few blossoms of any kind, except those of certain saprophytes which did not need light in which to grow, since they lived on dead wood in the soil—the snowy-white Indian pipe and the amber-pink pine sap, and that parasite, the pale beige of the beech drops springing up in late summer around the beech trees and growing from their roots. Now the white fruits of the baneberry were maturing on their carmine stalks, and the crimson baneberry also, while the blue fruits of the clintonia were a startling contrast. So were the scarlet bunchberries centered on their rosettes of low leaf-whorls, and the partridgeberries—more of that Christmas red and green. The stick-tight seeds of sweet cicely, hound's tongue, and Lappula poked their prongs into my clothing and went along with me.

LIGHT IN THE FOREST

On a sunny summer day, when the fields are sweet with the perfumes of clover and the warm scent of growing corn and ripening grain, and with the dark green of well-developed plants everywhere, absorbing the sun's heat and energy, the light in the forest is vital to its life. Yet, only about six per cent of the sunlight on a sunny day reaches the lower parts of the woods; and, I suppose, even less of it must reach the forest floor itself. This variation in light also produces a great variation in temperature as well, from top level to the ground, often a difference of many degrees.

Tremendous changes in the quality of light take place in the woods all around me. On a sunny day it is direct and strong, but much of it is bounced off into the atmosphere as reflection from the upper leaves, so that very little reaches the ground. It is difficult to take a snapshot here in the summer woods when the sun is out. On a cloudy day, the light seems to be gently diffused, and is actually more intense down below in the woods than it was on the sunny day. This diffusion is called sky light, a scattering of light in dust particles, molecules of gases, and droplets of moisture in the air. Even before I knew that the floor of the woods, by means of this sky light, received up to twenty per cent of the total light of the cloudy day, I had guessed it because of the availability of light for the camera.

It is the leaves which use the sunshine in order to bring its benefits to the tree. Wood and bark could take in little of it, but the leaf is fitted to absorb sunlight easily. Those in the tops of the trees are smaller and thicker than those below, and absorb as much as eighty per cent of the light. The lower leaves in the shade are usually broad and thin, to take advantage of the scantier illumination. They are arranged on the twigs so that no leaf is directly over another.

Leaves are wonderful in their work and complexity. So much is compressed into the leaf's thin green structure which is multiplied in such huge numbers on every living deciduous tree. The upper surface of the leaf is smooth or hairy, is waxy or leathery. It is covered with a single layer of cells which contain cutin, a waxy substance which is waterproof and from which dust will blow or wash away rather than be absorbed or clog the breathing pores. Through these invisible openings, the stomata, there is a constant exchange of oxygen and carbon dioxide between the cells of the leaf and the atmosphere, and the passage of water vapor from the leaf to the air. Cooling at night condenses this vapor; in the early morning the leaves drip with the result of this condensation—dew.

The inside of the leaf makes use of the sunshine after it is taken in through the windowpane of cutinized cells. The inner part is made of spongy cells held together by veins and laid out beneath the windowpane cells, to receive the sunlight. Here in the cells containing that green chemical stuff called chlorophyll there takes place that marvelous and not at all well understood process of making sugar from raw materials. When this process is very rapid, as it is in midsummer, too much sugar is made for the tree to use at once.

THE DECIDUOUS WOODS

During the day, therefore, much of it is changed to starch; and at night it is changed back into forms of sugar, mainly glucose, dissolved in sap, and carried away to the trunk. One leaf on a summer day may make at least one gram of glucose per square meter of leaf surface.

THE FLOOR OF THE FOREST

Down on the shadowy floor of the woods, soft with old leaf mold made by generations of foliage long since fallen in previous autumns—a dark and almost windless place—I found a world that was the haunt of millions of small plants and animals at whose presence, for the most part, I could only guess. Yet they led often interlocking lives on which hinged much of the whole life of the forest itself. They helped to make it a place of constant change, as they do in all woodlands, deciduous or coniferous, for life, death, and various forms of resurrection continually take place here. Because of these unseen hordes, no part of the woods or its underpinning is quite the same from one day to the next, even from one hour to the next, or between moments, for the changing goes on in all things. Sometimes it is rapid, as in the twenty-four hour growth and deterioration of a shaggy-mane mushroom in warm weather, or slowly, as in the life, death, and disintegration of a tree, or in the crumbling of a rock.

Many of the residents of the forest floor occupy themselves in cleaning up the dead organic material deposited there. Weather and time, through rain and erosion and the percolating action of water dripping through the leaf mold and earth, dispose of other dead creatures and vegetable matter. Bacteria are of first importance in breaking down organic material and returning it to the soil, but fungi, insects, and snails, by devouring it, pulverize, disintegrate, and reduce its elements.

The fungi are especially active in disposing of trash. From mycelium (white filaments of fungal thread) creeping under damp leaves or just beneath the surface of the friable earth or inside dead wood and crumbling old logs, mushrooms spring up. They produce their often gaudy parasols, brackets, coral forms, or other fascinating shapes, shed their spores, and often vanish quickly. But the mycelium meanwhile has eaten away more of the dead wood and has further reduced it a little more. Time means little in the forest. To dispose of an entire dead tree may take decades of attack by fungi and bacteria. Other plants and animals join in the assault.

When I walked through the woods I was little aware of this minute world of drama and life under my feet. The only way to see and begin to know it was to sit down on a log, pick up old leaves, then cautiously roll back the log to see what dwelt beneath it, afterward putting log and leaves back where they belonged. The tiny animals living beneath them were thus not exposed to light and danger; nor did I leave an untidy raw place in the woods. Using a hand lens on some of the small things I found here opened a whole new world on the floor of the forest.

It was all dependent upon that undisturbed yet ever changing leaf mold and the more recent clutter of old leaves and twigs, the fallen trees, the dead animals, seeds, bark, and other natural debris of the woods—a tremendous tonnage every year. The leaf mold holds warmth and moisture in itself. It reduces the wide range of temperature to be found outside the woods, and aids in the germination of seeds, the hatching of insects and the multiplying of many forms of life. It reduces the depth to which frost may penetrate in winter, is the insulation between winter's severity and the life in the earth. Bare soil may be frozen hard as rock, but under forest litter it remains porous and loose, especially when it has the snow as an additional insulation.

Because of the leaf mold, moisture is retained in a far greater amount than it is in bare ground in open sunshine. This material, far from being dead and useless trash, plays an important part not only in the lives of the trees and the general welfare of the woods. It constructs a miniature jungle, a gnomish wilderness of secrecy

THE DECIDUOUS WOODS

and shelter for those myriads of the small, often ferocious creatures which spend all their lives on or in the ground.

It was a world of miniatures around my feet, but all I needed was to change my perspective to begin to understand some of its immensities. Here were jungles of moss plants, closely set like a spruce forest half an inch high, some of the little "trees" topped with turban-shaped spore cases, a different shape for every moss. I used the lens on a spore case and saw the opening in the top arranged in overlapping teeth, like the trick box-tops created in paper by the Japanese. In one situation all the teeth overlapped in a circle, and the opening was closed. On pressure—or drying—the whole thing popped open, and the spores were thrown out in centrifugal motion.

There were curious little green growths of Marchantia liverworts with their small, dignified umbrellas of spore-bearing structures. There were some germinating maple seeds which had sent down a single root and put up a single stem with a pair of cotyledons and the first pair of leaves of an incipient forest tree. On a decayed log I found slime molds in a Persian carpeting of purple-red. Here the strange, two-existence slime mold had oozed like egg-white over the log, in definite motion and with food-absorbing ability. It had been transformed, perhaps only this morning, from its amoeba-like animal form to its colorful plantlike form. It had paused dramatically, had dried, changed, had become this rug-pile, this collection of tiny, closely-set, club-shaped structures poised upright like the plumes worn by circus horses, each set on a tenuous little stalk. A touch, and purple-red spore dust came off on my fingers.

Plant life, half-and-half life, animal life—in this miniature safari on a summer day I began to see what had been living here all the time. Not many, actually, were as apparent and visible as some—an angular daddy longlegs straddling across dead leaves; a small caterpillar climbing a twig; an empty white cocoon of the luna moth; the neat, beige-gray tree frog with gold rims around its eyes, so well concealed on old maple leaves that I might never have seen it at all. A spider making a funnel-web under some leaves zipped back into its protection when my hand came too close. A glittering green-and-scarlet tiger beetle went rattling along in a hunt for something to eat. There were some brown ants in a long, determined procession, going somewhere with the diligent intentness and determination of their kind. Dark-brown and shiny carpenter ants on assembly line were throwing grains of sawdust out of a small hole in the end of a log.

When I rolled back the log, no doubt dreadfully upsetting the creatures inside it, I found the old wood black and moist beneath, with a fine lacework of mushroom mycelium draped over portions of it. There were some Lenzites bracket fungi growing under it, greened with algae, as if they had been there for a long time but had once been out in the light—as if the log had been rolled over on them and they had continued to grow underneath. Also beneath the log lay three red oak acorns whose interiors had been eaten out by a wood mouse. There was a little heap of round gray basswood seeds, each one neatly halved and quite empty. Several glossy black beetles scurried out of sight; a brown millipede lay in a little channel in the decaying wood.

The log smelled woodsy, smelled of mushrooms and moss, and of the cool, moist odor of decaying wood and soft damp earth. Its fragrance was of the forest, part of its whole essence, part of the sequence of passing from life, to death, to change, to life again.

Exploring along the length of the old log, I caught a glimpse of something red and shiny and very fragile. It was a tiny newt, as delicate as some creation in varnished vermilion wax. It slid away, its bright black eyes intent on escape. It vanished under a shred of rotted wood, slipping no doubt into some private tunnel-way leading to the secret depths of the log, where perhaps many creatures I did not suspect lurked in darkness, dampness, and shelter.

From the evidence of old nutshells and seeds, the wood mice must have been here often, but one of them apparently had not

THE DECIDUOUS WOODS

lived to go on its way again. Perhaps a shrew had come foraging, had surprised the mouse at its dinner beneath the log, and had leaped, pierced the mouse's neck with needle teeth and injected poison into its bloodstream. Very quickly the mouse had died. I knew it had died—under the log there was a small, clean, white skull, punctured to remove the brain. The rest of the body had long since been taken away or devoured by beetles and other scavengers.

A snail shell had a hole in one side—the mouse had no doubt eaten the tender, succulent meat. Another snail was alive. In the summer warmth and dryness of the woods, it had retired into the cool darkness beneath the log, had sealed the shell's aperture with a film of mucous which had hardened to a covering almost like thin isinglass or plastic. It would remain sealed in with its own humidity until the rains came.

As I was turning the log back to its old seat, an amber centipede sprinted away from a point I had not investigated, and I knew that only by tearing apart the whole log, as the bears do to get at the ants inside, would I really know all that was part of its existence. I had no wish to upset and displace its inhabitants. They were all part of the full and complicated picture of the woods—a picture which ranged from the next year's buds already formed on the tips of the tallest tree-twigs to the lowest, to the multitudes of life-forms down in the leaf mold and earth, and under all the logs, with the flowers, fruits, tree trunks, birds, mammals, insects, reptiles, amphibians, and other creatures populating all parts of it, each to its own uses and ways.

CHAPTER NINE

WATER GARDENS

WHEN I rowed across the lake to the marshy bay, the August mists were still steaming from the water, and there were still some of the quietness and the smells of night. The water lilies were not yet open. The new flowers of the pickerel weed were just unfurling. They glistened like amethyst overlaid with silvery sparkles as the sunlight finally touched them. Life in the bay seemed to lie as in a dream, still half asleep in the cool shadows. As the sun topped the spruces and pines on the east shore, and touched each plant, it responded to light and opened wide. As if turned on by a clock—by the timepiece of the daily return of sunlight—flowers opened, insects awoke, and life picked up its tempo of the summer day.

WATER LILIES

As I pushed the boat into the beds of water lilies, little oval black seeds which had been drifting dully on the surface came alive, zipped over the sunlit water, and drew arcs and circles and long whiplash marks of speed—the whirligig beetles were out for food after a night of quiescence in the chill. Food—life—hurry—zip—swirl—get that fly—tear it up—fight over it—eat—zip—swirl! The beetles were animation in jet—keen-eyed hunters whose territory was the surface film; yet they might on occasion descend for some insect swimming in the depths. Equipped for just such activity, the whirlgigs had two eyes above and two below—or rather, their two eyes were divided into four, so they could see above and below at the same time.

Angular water striders set dimples in the surface film. They skated over it as if it were ice and had substance. They and the whirligigs dwelt in open water among the water lily leaves. I found these leaves torn, eaten, and old-looking, their work of the season almost done, their surfaces a record of what had come there or lived there or laid eggs on them during the summer. The leathery leaves had been ripped by paddles of boats; holes had been chewed by the bronzy Donacia beetles.

Earlier in the season I had watched a nervous female Donacia ranging over a leaf, then stopping to chew an oblong hole. Inserting her ovipostitor so that it curved not only into the opening but up to the underside of the leaf, she laid two or three rows of tiny, white cylindrical eggs around the hole. They were held securely by glue poured out by the insect at the time she laid the eggs; when the young hatched, they would fall to the bottom, where they would feed. They and their parents actually are air-breathing insects. The adults would not enter the water even to lay their eggs. Down in the lake the air-breathing young would hastily chew little holes in the pipes of the water lily stems and thrust in their heads. Thus, they could eat plant tissue and at the same time take in air brought down to them via the lily's conduits. Even when the larva is mature and must spin a little silken cocoon, it entraps air bubbles in the silk, so that when the beetle emerges it carries bubbles caught in the little hairs on its underside, enough *scuba* equipment to get it to the surface and out into the full burst of air and summer sunshine.

The Donacias were always a part of the lily beds. It seemed that whenever I came rowing in, or pushing in as quietly as possible with the canoe, the adults were always running about over the slick green platters of the leaves, or busily chewing more holes in the leathery surfaces.

The whole domain of the water lilies was well populated. The majority of the creatures using the undersides or the upper levels of the lilies would very likely not be here at all without the diverse kinds of support or shelter or food given by these plants. Dragonflies and damselflies hawked over the leaves and flowers after insects, or paused in a glitter of wings on leaf or bud, while below in the mud their larvae were feeding around the roots of the lily colony. Snails had laid gelatinous clusters of eggs beneath the leaves —eggs which were kept moist by the leaf's contact with the water and protected from the drying, burning effect of the direct sunshine while warmed by its heat coming through the insulating thickness of the leaf itself.

Leaning over the gunwale, I tugged at a tattered leaf. The boat rocked and tilted precariously before I could dislodge a four-foot length of stem which was extraordinarily tough and rubbery. Some of the inhabitants at once began getting off and tumbling back into the water—several small Physa snails, a water-boatman which had been clinging to it to hold itself down in the water, in order to feed on algae on the stem; a water scorpion and half a dozen frantic little twisting white worms departed hastily. The slippery stem was covered with a coating of diatoms and algae. The snails had clung to it, feeding. But I found none of the infant Donacias; they were evidently all grown and gone off by now into the world of the upper air. Sliced in cross-section, the stem showed the four air holes which are tubes, running the length of the stem to connect root with flower, pliable pipes often four feet long.

Around me floated the pure white blossoms of the water lilies, opening in the morning light and sending their fragrance into the warming sunshine. From the vantage point of the boat, I leaned over to examine the blossom itself which was buoyed by its pair of firm green sepals. These, on opening from the bud, had bent back so that their cupped forms rested like pontoons on the water and kept the flower from getting its pollen wet. The prime rule in most flowers—keep your powder dry.

The inner side of each sepal was white, for it was derived from the petals. In the water lily the sepals and petals and stamens seem to have merged one with the other. I could trace the petal-form from the inside of the sepal through the four rows of true petals. An inner row was tipped with yellow, as if already becoming stamens.

The stamens themselves looked like very narrow, modified petals. They surrounded in a quivering hedge the pepper-box pistil with its holes in the surface, through which thrust the short yellow stigmas. In the water lily, the stamens and pistil are on one flower, but they are ripe at different times to prevent any chance of self-pollination. The first day the flower opens just enough to permit entry of insects carrying pollen from a flower which had opened earlier. The bees and flies scramble over the conical pistil, leaving pollen on the stigmas. Next day the stamens of that flower are ripe, but the pistil will take no more pollen. Insects buzzing about in the fragrant cup dust themselves with the pollen which must be taken to another flower. When the blossom is finished, the pod bends down into the water where the seeds ripen and fall into the mud.

In water that was shallower than where the white lilies grew, I came into the massed beds of leaves of the yellow water lily, or cow lily, which has little of the charm of the white species, but which has its own place in the wild gardens of the waters. Its compact, close-furled, butter-yellow petals around a large barrel-shaped pistil follow the same rule as its more beautiful kin, opening only a little way on the first day in order to admit insects bearing pollen, then opening farther next day when its own stamens are bursting with pollen ready to be taken away. Its seed pod, like that of the white lily, bends down into the water for maturing. The seeds, therefore, are placed exactly where they must be for germination. Prolonged drying will destroy them. To prevent this and provide the softening power of immersion to open them next spring, the seeds of the Nuphar, the yellow water lily, as in Nymphaea, the white water lily, fall directly and efficiently into the mud.

Their larger, more spade-shaped leaves were very much tattered both by boats and insects. Channels had been carved in them by the leaf miners, the caterpillars of small aquatic moths called Nymphula. The adults are favorite fish food on a summer evening when they are flitting low over the water. I found where the caterpillar had chewed out small round or oval patches of lily leaves and had neatly fastened them together with silk to make a floating leaf case. These are sometimes fastened to the leaf itself by means of a strand of torn leaf-tissue, some float free, while others may be fastened to the underside of a leaf. Within its case the caterpillar lives in water and breathes by means of branched gills, meanwhile feeding on the leaf tissue in the protective case itself. At first, when the caterpillar is very young and its jaws are weak, it feeds only upon the more tender inner green cells. When it grows older and stronger, it devours the outside of the case and, having eaten bed and boat, is then ready to pupate.

Since there are usually two broods, those which come early in summer simply pupate in what is left of the leaf-cases fastened beneath the water lily leaves. The latter generation, which I now found in action, will sink into the water, hibernate among the old dead leaves of the water lilies, and be ready to climb up with the new, growing, red leaves in spring to start the cycle over again.

On the yellow lilies, as on the white, the Donacia beetles had laid eggs inside holes chewed in the leaves. In some places where the water level drops in summer, the leaves of the yellow species by August are left above water and become dry beneath. Since the Donacia eggs and larvae must be kept wet, the female then transfers her affections to the white water lily leaves which are more flexible and stay floating no matter what the level.

HORNWORT

Having left the entanglement of the water lily beds, and drifting gently in the direction of the shores of the little bay, I was now moving above thick underwater jungles of the hornwort and

Hornwort

eelgrass beds. Each depth of water seemed to have its own populations. The hornwort, or Ceratophyllum, floated in a dense congregation of unrooted, feathery, dark-green plants, which are often used in aquariums—and in this greater aquarium of the quiet bay it was the haunt of much wildlife which lurked in its green and ferny jungles. From the hank of the dripping green stuff pulled from the water, the inhabitants, at the shock of contacting air and sunlight, began to depart in a great hurry and drop back into the water. Tiny snails and worms, a couple of baby crayfish, a back-swimmer, and half a dozen nymphs of damselflies all went back to the water before I laid the plants on the boat-seat. There was something else in the vegetation which was a good deal more enormous than the rest of the small denizens of the world of the hornwort. Cautiously, I separated the wet strands and brought out a two-inch larva of the dobson fly. The adult is a large flying insect of the summer night, while the grotesque larva, called hellgrammite by fishermen, who find it an excellent bait for bass, lives for three years in the hornwort beds before becoming adult.

In the axils of the ferny whorls of thin-cut hornwort leaves there were remains of very tiny greenish flowers which never get above water. In order to pollinate the female flowers, the stamens themselves are released from the plant and are buoyed to the surface. Here they float about for a bit before showering into the water the grains of pollen. These are heavy enough to sink eventually and so come in contact with the pistillate flowers down below on the floating plants.

The hornwort broke apart easily. From each piece a new plant would grow. As autumn nears, the ends of the branches, the newest portions, break off naturally. They float about for a while, usually on the surface, and finally settle for the winter on the bottom of the lake. Part of this pull to the bottom is exerted by the load of animals riding on the hornwort fragments—the insects and their larvae, the nematode worms, the tiny young clams, midge larvae, and crayfish. When spring comes, the hornwort floats again. It soon sends out more branches to make new plants which form floating colonies, like the Sargassum weed in the Caribbean off Bermuda and, like it, occupied by a myriad population of animals.

EELGRASS

In more open patches of water where the hornwort did not dominate, other plants did. Here the eelgrass, rooted in the mud, sent up long, ribbon-like leaves that waved in the current. Vallisneria, the eelgrass, deeply submerged, nevertheless has, like most water plants, the need to get its flowers above the level of the water, out into the air and sunshine, so that they may be fertilized. It is a vital act which is accomplished in many ways by the water plants. The hornworts themselves set up curious oscillating movements to increase the chance that pollen will reach the submerged stigmas. In the Zannichellia, another submerged plant in the lake, a thin layer of tissue forms a tiny funnel around the stigma, so that the pollen may be more easily brought to where it is needed.

But the eelgrass, aquatic throughout its life, still must be fertilized on the surface of the water. Male and female flowers are borne on separate stalks. When the pistillate flower is ready to be pollinated, the long, wiry, or thready stalk, coiled into a corkscrew spiral near the base of the plant, is unfurled just far enough to get it to the top. Here the flower bursts open. It is a conspicuous little thing with its three broad, spreading, stigmatic lobes, each one cleft at the top and fringed along the edges. It is rather like a very tiny, very fancy trillium floating on the water.

The male flower is also sent by an unfurling spring-wire coil to the surface, where the spathe suddenly pops open and throws out a shower of flower buds on the water. Buoyed by an air bubble so that it floats nicely, each flower's tiny calyx bends back to make little pontoons. The anthers quickly open to expose the pollen whose large and sticky grains cling together. When some of these come into contact with the waiting female flowers, the white pollen is left on them as the little boats touch briefly and then drift on again.

They were floating all about me that day, got themselves stuck on the oars or lay where they had been tossed on water lily leaves by the backwash of motor boats out in the open lake, and of course were quite lost to any use. But the eelgrass produces so many of these buoyant pollen boats that a few lost ones make little difference.

When the pistillate flower has received its pollen, the plant responds and immediately hauls in the line. The coil is retracted and brought into the depths again, where the seeds form. These, later on, are released in the water and fall to the mud where they grow. For only a brief moment, Vallisneria has known the sun.

JOURNEYS IN GREEN PLACES

STUMP GARDENS

As the boat drifted sharply against a stump, a pair of splashes marked the departure of two frogs. A painted turtle on a floating log, no doubt watching my approach, slid quickly into the water. Stump and log, frog and turtle, announced that I had indeed come into another part of the bay with its own forms of life and its own unmistakable characteristics.

Many years ago, this lake and its connecting chain of lakes had been added to the great northern flowage system by which water is held in reserve to supply the Mississippi watershed. In the subsequent rise in water level, the spruces once growing in a marsh were submerged. They finally died as the rising lake level stood several feet high around their bases. The dead wood, in time, finally gave way and fell into the water. Thus, the shallows were filled with remains of old stumps and with long, lean, floating trees whose branches are now long since worn away, although the location of each one is still marked by a hard, sharp stub.

The stumps and many of the floaters had become a series of little water gardens, miniature islands of concentrated life. There were, however, two real islands in the deeper water just outside the water lily zone. They may have originally been high ground beside the lake, but in being surrounded by the rising waters, they had become islands. They were so small and lay so close to the water that they immediately became planted with a few swamp spruces, sweet gale, and leatherleaf. They had now reached their maximum population with plants which were packed so tightly on the small available space that there was little or no room left for anyone to land. But they were islands, and they had names, no doubt unrecorded, but nevertheless names. Two little boys who vacationed near here once claimed them on a canoeing expedition with their grandfather. One is Quint's Island; the other is Mike's Island.

It was a good deal easier to explore the miniature stump islands than these larger ones. I was continually bumping into the stumps, or crunching over another submerged one. Each stump had a small assortment of special plants, often one of a kind in half a dozen varieties. One had a little spruce tree growing out of its top, a miniature Christmas tree a foot tall. The surface of this stump and its sides were all neatly covered with moss which, although exposed to hot sunshine most of the day, evidently drew enough moisture through the dead wood to remain fresh. In the moss I found some birch seedlings an inch tall, another young spruce no more than two inches in height, a purple-flowered skullcap plant in full bloom, a plant of marsh St. John's wort with its polished maroon stems and seed pods, several jewelweed plants, one beginning to bloom. It held suspended over the amber water a number of dangling orange eardrop flowers. A whir, a flash, a glitter—a hummingbird had come out from the woods, had probed three orange flowers, and had gone again. This whole garden on the stump occupied an area of about a foot in diameter and stood eight inches above the water.

Another stump had a tuft of marsh grass and one violet plant. Still another was a pincushion of sundews. A stump with moss, skullcap, and a small goldenrod had a silken net spread over part of it, narrowing to a funnel. A large brown wolf spider half the size of my palm lurked in it. And down in the water beside the stump were other creatures which looked so plantlike that the resemblance to any sort of animal was difficult to see.

SPONGES

Sponges—green sponges. Attached to the lower part of the stump and to dead branches lying submerged nearby, they waved in the motion of the water. They were handsome, as sponges go, a tribe not especially noteworthy for beauty. Many of those in fresh water are simply "globs of goo," as a child once stated succinctly and with no admiration whatever. These, however, were soft masses of material which might resemble bundles of closely packed, curled green hair, fastened at one end to the dead wood, or coating it as with a thick smear of bright-green paint. Those in deep shade or beneath the fallen logs were brownish and not so handsome. In sunny water, it was the algae which were responsible for that beautiful green which dressed up even the lowly sponge.

Sponges must have clear, clean water, and they found it in the bright northern lake. Their very presence indicated purity. Sponges consist of colonies of animals living together in a soft substance which is a skeleton made up of a lattice-like supporting framework composed of transparent, very small soft needles called spicules. They are made of silica and are different in shape in each kind of sponge. I might (if I were so industrious) identify the species by the shape of these little needles alone. I preferred at that moment to lean over the edge of the boat and gaze down through the glass-clear water at the green sponges waving below; it was enough for me to know how they were formed and what they were doing down there.

There were holes in these creatures, small holes called osteoles, and larger ones called oscula. Water was being sucked in by the osteoles, and forced out through the larger openings, the whole purpose of this endless in-and-out business being to bring food to the sponge. As the flow of water carrying minute animal life moved into the sponge's gastral chamber, the food matter was digested and waste matter swept out of the oscula. A "glob" though it may appear, the sponge was simply a hungry colonial animal obtaining food for itself in this life-filled haunt of the lake. So life-filled was it that even the sponge had dwellers within its colony.

The strange little parasitic larvae of the Spongilla flies find food within the sponge itself. The larvae are incessantly hungry little things, and the sponges have no defense against them. These enemies go down into the osteoles and chew their way into the sponge cells. They suck out their contents—actually suck, as if through a sort of straw—for the mandibles are hollowed on the inner side. Poking this tube into a cell, the insect drains out the liquid contents, then moves on to another convenient dish of sponge soup. Because it is so much the color of its food, the Spongilla larva is all but invisible until it moves.

PICKEREL WEED

I had caught only a glimpse of the pickerel weed off near the shore when I first came into the bay, and now my boat was among the tall, tropical-looking plants standing above the water. I never realized how beautiful the glistening lilac flowers of the pickerel weed could be until that morning. They were just opening. Always before, it seemed that I had come later in the morning, after they had already lost their freshness and had begun to curl and fade a little. Although the spike of flowers held that splendid lilac-blue-

Pickerel weed

purple color all day long, the close-up view was always something of a disappointment. For that matter, for a long time I had had no idea of the true shape of the flower. Pictures in botany manuals showed them to be pretty well curled, as if they were never any different. These were pictures, I now concluded, which had been drawn by people who never got up early enough to see the pickerel weed in full, early bloom on a beautiful summer morning.

Now I could see how the Pontederia could claim kinship with its glorious, if unpopular, tropical relative, the water hyacinth, which fills bayous and lakes in Louisiana, Florida, and other parts of the far south. Here was that same glistening sparkle of the flowers, a sparkle caused by an outer layer of infinitely thin, clear cells, as in the orchids, which picked up light and refracted it like jewels over the petals. Here were six flower parts—three above, three below— each upper petal marked with a splendid canary-yellow spot surrounded as by a dark, purple-blue halo. Dozens of flowers bloomed at once on the spike which also held many forming seeds and downy, silvery buds which had not yet opened.

Pickerel weed flowers have three kinds of stamens and pistils, the long, medium, and short, and each length is found in different flowers scattered throughout the colony. It was Charles Darwin's experiments with these plants which first revealed their curious story. He found that pollen from long stamens must fertilize long pistils, just as pollen from the medium or short stamens must fertilize the medium or short pistils. For, as the bee enters the flower, the pollen from the stamens, whichever length may be in that particular flower, touches the head, the chest, or the abdomen of the bee; it all depends upon how long the stamens are! As the bee goes into other flowers, the long, medium, or short pistils touch whichever spot of pollen came from those particular-length stamens. It is a complicated way in which to insure healthy seeds, the pickerel weed's way.

I could also see, on this August morning, how the high-held seeds were put into the water where they must ripen, rather than in the upper air. Finished with their long blossoming period, some of the three-foot stalks, like long, muscular arms, were now bending over and carrying the seed-heads down into the water. Some were already submerged; others were on the way down. The flowering stalks, however, were still high above the big spade-shaped, dark-green leaves, waiting for those discriminatory bees carrying pollen from short, medium, or long stamens for the short, medium, or long pistils.

BUR REEDS AND ARROWHEADS

As the boat drifted closer to the shore, I came among still another colony of plants which stood in less than a foot of water: the bur

Arrowhead

reeds, the bulrushes, and the arrowheads. Some of the bur reeds, bearing polleny puffballs of pale-yellow and white flowers which seemed to be all stamens or all pistils, stood in upright colonies well above the water. Another species apparently could not get its leaves to stand upright, so they had become adapted to a thoroughly aquatic life. They were long ribbons of leaves, often five feet long, which rose only to the surface and then streamed out on the water, all in the same direction when wind or current guided them. They made intricate patterns on the surface, studded now and again with short stalks of flower balls which just cleared the water and managed to stand six inches above it. Curious little fluffy heads standing among their long, dramatic, streaming leaves, they sometimes gave me the feeling that they were beings which were faintly supernatural—like Disney elves emerging to dance strange, twirling dances at sundown along the ribbon pathways of their leaves.

There were among them also the slender little red-brown stalks of small arrowhead lilies. Here were compactness and simplicity, one or two clean-carved, arrow-shaped leaves standing several inches above the water, and one slender, erect, red-brown stalk which bore three or four shining white, ruffled, three-parted blossoms—the arrowhead lily rising in splendid economy from its submerged tuber.

The brief stalk has segregated areas. The blossoms in the lower whorl are pistillate, their centers a tight cluster of carpel points. Those in the whorl above have ball-clusters composed only of yellow stamens. It would seem that the upper flowers must only be shaken a trifle by the wind to drop pollen on the waiting pistils beneath, but this would be too easy and not to be desired. The arrowhead, like most flowers, eschews self-pollination. Thus when the pistillate blossoms are ready for pollen, the upper flowers on that particular stalk have not opened. Therefore, some pollen must be brought from flowers on another plant. This pollination is carried out by two most unlikely tribes of creatures—by the dragonflies and damselflies, and by water snails. The latter climb up on the stalks in search of a favorite delicacy—the petals of the arrowhead. In getting this delightful, snowy salad, and in going from plant to plant for more, the snails evidently carry pollen on their mucilaginous bodies. The dragonflies and damselflies, which are forever hawking about among the arrowheads and bur reeds after the mosquitoes common there, come down on the plants to rest. It is known that they, too, carry pollen from arrowhead to arrowhead, and perhaps they do this for the bur reeds also. They do not eat the flowers or even seek the nectar, but, simply through accidental contact, they serve their purpose to Sagittaria, the arrowhead.

Farther south, the arrowheads grow very large and form dense jungles of waist-high leaves in backwater lakes and sloughs near rivers. This simple little arrowhead beside my boat, alone and perfect and small in the bay of a northern lake, had a charm which far outreached those elegant, rank species growing down the valley of the Mississippi River.

THE OTTER AND THE HERON

It was a concentrated area of plant and animal life. I did not need the presence of the great blue heron to tell me that life of many sorts abounded, nor did I need the unseen presence of the otter which might even then be watching curiously from the doorway of a burrow in the bank behind the marsh grass.

One evening at dusk I had come over to the bay, paddling the canoe so slowly in the twilight that even the otter had failed to notice my coming. I drifted, watching, as the long, lithe animal poised itself at the top of a little slope above the water where spruce roots hung, then launched itself down a muddy slide it had created for its own pleasure. The otter hit the water with a joyous, slithering splash. It paddled out and was up again, when some whiff of an alien watcher sent it quickly into the water and no doubt into a hidden hole. It was too dark for me to be sure where it went; but I knew it lived in the marshy bay, where I had seen it fishing once or twice from a log. I felt that it was very likely watching me. Then the heron, four feet tall and as gaunt as a tree snag in the shadows, had opened its great wings and, with a guttural squawk, flapped low across the darkening water, over the closed-up water lilies, past the two islands, and on across the width of the lake.

THE WATCHERS

I frequently had the agreeable feeling of being watched when I came here, not only by the wary-eyed turtles and frogs and the kingbirds charging out from a dead spruce after insects, but also by deer, and owl, and bear. It was a private sort of place, much too shallow and cluttered with stumps and logs and plants to entice motor boats. It was a place where fishermen seldom came. With the canoe or rowboat I could ease my way in to the quiet haunt of heron and otter, of fish and sponge and water beetle, of turtle and frog and of whatever else lurked in water or on land.

I knew that bears sometimes came down to the shores to drink. I had seen bold and exciting tracks imprinted in muddy sand below the bank at a point where I once had beached the canoe to come ashore and explore the woods for orchids. I had not seen the bear, but could almost hear his grunting "oof!" as he had evidently come down off the bank onto his forefeet, which had left tracks deeply imprinted with his weight. Simply to know that I was in the domain of the bear was a stirring sensation. Not far away on the trail, inland from the bay, I had indeed come upon bears at times. They very likely knew the inlet and the surrounding forests a good deal better than I.

Deer also came to the shores to drink. From the evidence of cloven tracks, some broad and splayed, others neat and sharp, and the tiny prints of the fawns, I knew they came often. One day I had felt something watching as I sat in the canoe. Sometimes I think we never have lost all of our innate wilderness sense, those facets of our primitive character supposedly long forgotten in today's living. It told our ancestors when wild animals were near, or when a change was coming in the weather, or when a snake was lying along the other side of a fallen log. Frequently those invaluable aids to knowledge fail us, but many a time I knew they had come to my rescue for enlightenment. They came now. I looked in the right direction—looked where instinct told me to look.

Up the slope, lit by the low, orange-gold light of the setting sun coming through the woods, and blurred a little in the mists wreathing around their legs and among the ferns, stood a large red doe with half-grown twin fawns. They simply stood and gazed with a wide-eyed wonder at the silent canoe. We stared easily at each other for a long, sweet interlude, with the simplicity of the forest dusk uniting us one with the other in a bond of mutual tolerance. And then the doe, without any alarm, whiffled through her nose, flicked her tail, and turned. The fawns, with a backward glance of great curiosity over their smooth, red-brown shoulders, followed her through the ferns, walking, not running. They were gone, but it seemed as if I could still see them there in the milky shaft of the last rays of sundown and the mists of twilight. Whenever I pass that place today, remembering, it is almost as if they were still there.

I am no doubt like that hopeful hound who chases a rabbit into a hole and forever afterward sniffs there when he passes by, just in case the rabbit might have returned. Wherever I have seen bear or deer or porcupine or otter or raccoon or skunk, I always expect, confident as the hound, to find them there again.

They were as much a part of the quiet bay as the animals and plants in the waters themselves. In the water, however, it is the plant populations which seem most influential in determining the presence or absence of the animal life. When there are no yellow water lilies, there are no Nymphula moths; no white water lilies, no Donacia beetles; no hornwort, no snails, no fish. It is the plant populations which give food and lodging for the animals.

It is a wet world of life which is endlessly fascinating. I discover almost as much of the lure which the sea diver finds in the depths of his coral reef or his sea-botton with its shipwrecks. In a lesser way, I can find some creatures and plants which are kin to marine species—the great bryozoan, Pectinatella, as compared with bryozoans in the sea; the fresh-water sponges as compared with the marine varieties; the fresh-water snails and clams and crayfish and fishes, which have their counterparts in salt water; and the plants which remind me of diverse forms of seaweed but which, in the main, belong to much higher orders of plants. In a boat, I can float suspended on the surface of this world of water, at times using a glass jar or a dip net to bring up bits of its inhabitants to examine them further. The same lure and the same air of mystery of things not seen and of sounds not heard, which I find in the woods, I find here in the quiet bay and lake on a summer evening.

CHAPTER TEN

THE ALCHEMY OF AUTUMN

THE morning was filled with a stirring fragrance. It was late autumn in the north—mid-October—and most of the leaves had fallen; yet their perfume remained more potently strong than ever. The red maples had begun to crimson in August, then had dallied, coloring here and there in sudden splashes of red on the summer landscape until September. A great burst of pure scarlet had then surged along roads and through woods and swamps, and had as quickly gone. Cold, wind, and rain had whipped off the leaves like bright flags and had flung them on the ground where, somewhat muted yet still colorful, they lay in a multihued carpet. Their white-frosted undersides were accents which only added to the pink-scarlet and crimson of the upper parts.

The sugar maples had then come to full glory, until a storm stripped most of them. The landscape was different once more; yet

THE ALCHEMY OF AUTUMN

in its own way it was no less beautiful. I could see for long distances where I could not see far before. Behind trees which I had driven past all summer, I discovered a lake whose presence I had not suspected. Water glimmered behind bare trees. Distant views of balsam spires and naked birch woods so altered the summer and early-autumn landscape that I could scarcely believe it was all the same countryside.

To walk among the bare white birches was almost a renewal of those bare spring woods, yet with a difference. There were no spring flowers now, and no small new leaves. Everything was finished. The chaste, chalky trunks, accented with their black scars, and the long brown switches of twigs on the upper branches gave an openness and a lightness even on a lowering day. Under them lay the fading gold-brown of their leaves. Bracken ferns had long since browned and bent over, but the maidenhair made chartreuse-green clumps of delicate fernery. The wood ferns were still as deep an emerald green as in summer, and they seemed twice as bright as when that hue was no rarity but the abundant color of life. Late autumn brought a distinctly different set of values and a new means of rating a landscape which was heading into the winter. It was revelatory and delightful. It was as if the autumn's changes had opened a door to new vistas which I had found no way to unlatch before. I could find no mournfulness here, no regret for lost leaves and flowers and birds. All about me were the living promises of next year's leaves and blossoms. They were packaged small and well-enwrapped for safest keeping.

There were still many colors. Here and there some aspens held their bright-gold doubloons in their upper branches. The slim trees were like golden plumes whose disk leaves shook incessantly in the wind and splashed a dazzling yellow against an October sky. Yet the leaves were coming down in a hurry. Every sudden gust caught and tossed them swirling into the air like confetti before they came at last to the ground. Out in the bogs, the tamaracks, one of the latest of all the trees to turn color, were changing—transformed almost over night as the urgency of autumn increased—to stand in slender pyramids of bronzy gold. Sigurd Olson, a noted Minnesota naturalist, calls them *smoky gold*, and, try as I might, I surely cannot find a better metaphor for these tamaracks in October.

But that fragrance, that incredible fragrance which met me as I opened the cabin door that morning and stepped out into the damp, cool world of October, reminded me of the aroma of sherry wine that has stood a little while in a glass. Yes, that was it, sherry. I could now understand the rather preposterous and poetic notion of writers of the past who spoke of the autumn air as "winey." Winey it really was, I knew now, like golden-brown cream sherry itself. That perfume emanated from the miles of damp autumn leaves lying on the ground, distilling from their spent food-matter and their chemicals this compounded aroma. Old pine needles sent up their own scent—it was all blended into that golden-brown perfume on a day of golden-brown trees, while a golden-brown partridge with an elegant fantail paraded past me through the open birch woods.

The partridges dwelt in woods which might be losing the current crop of verdure, in which life for the season might appear to be finished, but which was certainly far from being dead or ever really ended. Nature seldom completes anything totally. Except perhaps when certain species are permitted to become extinct, there is hardly ever a period put to the end of any sentence. There may be what appears to be an end; but it is really only a long rest or a semicolon, and after a time life resumes.

In spite of autumn's disposal of much of its greenery, there were still, aside from the coniferous trees which seemed much brighter than they had been all summer, a good many leaves in these woods which would remain green all winter. They were on the low plants of wintergreen and partridgeberry, the mosses, some of the ferns, the pipsissewa, pyrola, snowberry, ground pines, bearberry, and Labrador tea around the edge of the bog. In the bog itself were

THE ALCHEMY OF AUTUMN

the Cassandra, laurel, Andromeda, cranberry, even pitcher plant's leaves, and sphagnum, all retaining the green of summer. They were all fitted for a green survival during a weather interval in which many other kinds of leaves could not exist and so would have long since fallen, their work done, with next year's leaves prudently provided for.

The very presence of the unfading greenery, the falling away of golden leaves, the color itself, the perfume, all provoked questions which I had a hard time trying to explain. I could perhaps comprehend some of the chemist's explanations—for autumn indeed is a vast chemical laboratory—but the intricate reasons behind the explanations are not so easily understood.

COLOR

Long ago, I suppose, the autumns must have been a good deal more simple to know and to explain than they are today. They were an esthetic experience, not so much a display of complicated chemical and botanical truths. Yesterday we could gaily exclaim: "Look! Jack Frost came last night and painted all the leaves!" Today, in order to explain autumn and to understand only some of its marvels, I have to know something of plant anatomy and biochemistry, which are maybe not as romantic, but are inconceivably more fascinating. Each explanation of something hitherto unknown, or long ignored, opens for me another door to a wider wonder of the world.

Jack Frost may be forever lost as a painter of leaves, but the magic which replaces him is worth the exchange of fiction for fact. For the autumn is truly exciting. It is as splendid as any epic or saga. It is ten times more rewarding than any folk tale which left so many questions unanswered in a pleasant vagueness sopped in a syrup of ignorance.

There are always so many questions which I must ask before autumn is gone. Why do the trees turn color? How can plants live all winter? Why do some leaves fall and others remain? How do the trees come alive again in spring? How can spring flowers come into blossom after the devastating experience of great cold? Yet, in finding partial answers for these questions, I always come upon more which are still unexplained. It would be a pity if they were all answered and there were no more questions, no more queries, no more inexplicable wonders. Knowledge is good, but wonder is priceless. The one is of the mind, the other of the spirit.

Autumn means change. It means ripening. It means color which comes as part of the change, as a result of the ripening. Autumn is transition, and it must, at the same time, provide for the continuity of all life; it must provide a bridge which leaps the gap of winter to spring.

Life in its various ways has provided its means of survival, and autumn, late autumn, only serves as the serene transition. It removes tons of dead leaves from the trees, and puts them on the ground as an insulator between plants and the coming snow. It eventually will see to it that the old leaves are pulverized and disintegrated into a rich humus in the woods. There is a nice clearing away and a brooming out of debris in autumn. It was one of the purposes of that day's brisk wind which was rolling leaves down into ravines and piling them around tree trunks, sweeping them out of roads where they have no use, until the trees stood clean and bare and the old leaves lay neatly fastened down (to begin their long process of disintegration) under the moisture of autumn rains.

All summer those leaves had been making starches, some of which had been changed into soluble sugars and piped out of the leaves and down the stems. Plant sugars went into the process of ripening and sweetening the summer's fruits. They sweetened the wild raspberries and serviceberries, put the sugar in next spring's maple sap, and at the same time helped to bring about the red in certain autumn leaves. Red leaves are caused by a high concentration of that sugar, usually glucose, left in leaf cells after the remainder has been sent down to be stored in the trunk. There must be the chemi-

THE ALCHEMY OF AUTUMN

cal anthocyanin, along with a nitrogen deficiency, light, dryness, and a lowering of temperatures, especially at night. When all these requirements are met, plus the inherited tendencies of certain plants to become red, the flame of autumn flares forth.

In yellow and orange leaves, the combination is a different one. The chemicals to make these were present in the green leaves all summer, but were hidden in the concentration of green. When the chlorophyll vanishes as the leaf's work is done, then the carotin and xanthophyll glow yellow and orange in the autumn sunshine.

The sugars not only contribute to color formation; they also provide in some plants a certain ability to endure cold. This is one of the marvelous arrangements of nature in a climate which may vary between over ninety degrees in the summer to forty degrees below zero in winter. Today, as I write this, the news report has come that it is now forty-three degrees F. below zero in the very place where I walked on that fragrant autumn day several months ago.

The adaptability of plants to changing temperatures is very great. Sap in wood and leaves will naturally freeze and expand in extreme cold, and the cells may burst, or the protoplasm will coagulate. When the cold is too great or too sudden, the damage would be far greater if many plants did not carry their own antifreeze solution in the cytoplasm of their cells.

There is no need, of course, to protect the leaves which are falling down in autumn; these are finished. They are expendable trash and are not to be saved. But I am thinking of the multitudes of those small evergreen leaves in woods and bogs, and of the needles of the coniferous trees. Many evergreens, including the wintergreen, laurel, Labrador tea, and bearberry, are supplied with quantities of glucose rather than with starch, and this sugar protects the plant's protoplasm from damage in low temperatures. The early-growing plants, such as tulips, hyacinths, trout lilies, dutchman's breeches, and crocuses, also have much sugar in their leaves which can withstand hard freezes up to a little more than twenty-four hours before the frozen sap finally destroys the cells. The evergreen needles of the conifers and the leaves of birch and wild cherry are fortified with oil droplets which are an even greater protection than sugar from extreme and enduring cold.

This supply of oil has made it possible for the plants of high altitudes and high latitudes to endure the severe climates of these places. It was effective and was perhaps developed during the periods of extensive geologic glaciation when temperatures were lowered the year around and the more tender plants moved south or perished. Sugar and oil are both commonly found in most plants whose leaves live through the northern winter. They were, besides, protected by their leathery or waxed surfaces, their inrolled structure—perfected in the coniferous needle—and their small size, to present as tiny a surface as possible to drying effect of winter winds.

In both evergreen and deciduous plants lay the supreme proof of next year's life, the result of this year's proper planning and production. While the leaves were making food and the tree was adding a new layer of living tissue just under the bark—the layer which, in cross-section, would appear as a growth ring marking one year in the tree's life—the growing tips of every twig were extending another length of wood. In some trees farther south—the tree of heaven, the cottonwood, or the paulownia—this annual lengthening of twigs might be as much as three feet. In the little snowberry of the north, growth for the year may be a sixteenth of an inch. But the expansion is there. At the time of this growth, the cells just above where each leaf joined the twig produced a bud. This was at first very small—almost microscopic in the snowberry. By the time autumn came and the leaves were ripening and falling, these buds of the summer were large and well formed, insulated, sealed, waxed, varnished, ready to endure any weather. In each bud lay the picture of next year—the embryo of leaves, flowers, and growth cells, next year's complete supply. The buds were arranged on the twigs according to their traditional plan—alternate, as in basswood, beach, and aspen; opposite, as in maple, viburnum, and dogwood.

These were facts, marvelous facts which added to the glory of the serene and silent autumn woods. But the smell—that sherry smell of the autumn! For this, too, I had to find an explanation. To people accustomed to city smells which are often far from agreeable —automobile exhausts, stench from burning trash, oil fumes, factory odors, smog—the pure perfumes of the wild are half intoxicating in their unbelievable sweetness and spice. The warm scent of the sunshine on fallen pine needles is something we wish to capture. This is a far from original thought—Thoreau himself, long ago, when the American air over cities was not as heavily polluted as it is now, felt this when he exclaimed:

"Morning air! If men will not drink of this at the fountainhead of the day, why, then, we must even bottle some up and sell it in the shops, for the benefit of those who have lost their subscription ticket to the morning time of the world."

AROMA OF AUTUMN

This aroma of the autumn leaves, in particular, I find to be one of the rich and splendid experiences of the year. Even in summer, the scents are there, distinguishably different in each kind of tree— in oak and in elm (different, too, between white elm and slippery elm), in willow and in sycamore, in maple and in walnut. Just writing their names brings their special smells clearly to mind, for each kind of leaf has its own odor. Some are not so easily discerned by our often untrained and blunted senses of smell; others are more distinctive and part of our indelible impressions of the wild.

The memory of a particular odor or its recurrence is enough to bring a surge of nostalgia for a past which may have held the perfumes of arbutus or arbor vitae, balsam needles or ripe oak leaves. Leaf smells, however, seem to become most distinct in autumn. The air then is full of scents which have been distilled from the organic vapors given off by every leaf and flower during the entire growing season just past. It is these which contain enough concentrated perfume to give us that fresh smell every morning. They are the perfumes of autumn, with the attendant blue haze lying mysteriously in the air and blurring the distant view.

THE BLUE HAZE

That blue haze itself may be caused by those same scented vapors which are given off by all vegetation. Some vapors are volatile oils called terpenes; those given off by pine or balsam forests, which give the air in coniferous regions its delicious smell, are called pinenes. The fragrances of the autumn leaves themselves come from terpenoid compounds thought to have come from the decomposing red and yellow pigments, the carotinoids. It has been estimated that a million tons of these amazing volatile substances may be given off in a single year by the land plants of the world—by meadow grass and clover fields, by orchards and orange groves, by sage brush and pine trees, by deciduous forests, and by every leaf and every fragrant flower in the year. What a massive perfume! No wonder I thought I smelled sherry this morning. It had been fermented by the aspen leaves, mingled with the pine and balsam pinenes, compounded by the autumn rain and the needle-filled earth itself, to become the distilled aroma of autumn.

But the blue haze—it and the perfumed air are both produced by the compounds given off by all the green-growing stuff in the world. In certain places—and particularly predominant in the middle west, which is a land of greenery, and across the forested north—a blue haze in the air is always present in growing periods, and by late summer and autumn it becomes more concentrated. We used to think the haze was made by the smoke of burning leaves. The old legend was that it came from the ghosts of Indian campfires, a lovely legend which belongs with the myth of Jack Frost painting the leaves.

I could see the blue haze across the tamarack bog, blurring lavender around the bronze-gold feathers of the tapering trees, could see it off across the far horizon, lying in a dreamy sort of wistful afterthought of summer around the pinnacles of the black-green spruces.

Perhaps it really was an afterthought of summer. The blue haze, according to Dr. Fritz Went, of the St. Louis Botanical Garden, may be caused by the partial oxidation of those same aromatic oils, the terpenes and pinenes. It seems a logical solution—the oils, condensed into large molecules which refract blue light, make the haze of the American autumn.

The blue haze and the autumn perfume—they are both the distillation of long, golden weeks of summer and the ripening of leaves. I suppose the theory of the molecules and the oil droplets is a reasonable enough explanation for both, but it was much too matter-of-fact for a delirious morning in October, when I had just stepped from the cabin into a golden-brown world flavored with wine and balsam. I only knew that I was smelling aromas which had been forming all summer, and that in itself was explanation enough. And everywhere I walked, I could see reason and order and plan in the accomplishment of the autumn condition, the preparation for the imminent winter, and, perhaps even more important, for the coming of spring.

Winter was indeed very near. Before the morning fog burned from the meadow where the winding path of Nine Mile Creek had marked itself in a swathing of white mist, frost had glistened on the grass-blades and on the wild-rose fruits. It was chill—the night temperature had dropped to twenty-eight degrees, but had risen again too quickly for anything to be frozen. Not that there was much left to be damaged. The tender things were gone. The bracken ferns had turned brown even before there had been a frost. It had been a strange thing to see it happen. Until mid-August the bracken in the woods and along the forest roads, in sun and in shade, had remained large and stout, with broadly spreading, triangular, dark-green fronds. Here and there were a very few yellowing leaves. Then suddenly, as if overnight, all the bracken had turned bright yellow. Two days later it had browned and bent over. The bracken had simply reached the terminus of its existence for this year, had perished because of too few hours of light, rather than from the cold. In the ground, its multitudes of traveling roots were alive and set with buds which would put up new fronds in spring.

THE PREPARATION

Thus it is that even before any freeze comes plants and animals are ready. Long before any changes are visible, they have been under way for weeks. Unknown and unnoticed, the places where tree leaves met the twigs have been sealing themselves off. As a result of shorter hours of light, a waxy or corky layer of infinite thinness has been shutting off the xylem and phloem tubes which all summer had been pumping raw materials or carrying away sugars and starches. With these passages closed, the leaves have received no more water. They have begun to die and, in so doing, have changed. In a silent explosion of color, autumn has moved across the north. At the point where each leaf had been sealed off from the twig, a separation has taken place, and the leaves, in showers or singly, have been sent off at last.

Now in the silent woods no wind was stirring and not a chickadee or Canada jay or woodpecker called. A single yellow aspen leaf detached itself lightly from a twig and dipped and floated and curvetted until it rested on the ground among other leaves on which last night's fog droplets still glistened. Aspen leaves lay gently on the beds of wintergreen with their red berries, on the durable bluegray fluff of the reindeer lichens, and beneath the tiny flames of scarlet buds on the tips of the bare blueberry twigs. The trailing arbutus was hidden beneath fallen leaves, but I could still find it and saw, enclosed in green and brown husks, the fully formed, large flower buds for next spring. I could see white petals peering out of the sepal husks, but knew they would have to stay where they were, dormant under snow, for a long time. Six months or more from this autumn day, I might again come here, turn back the moist leaves, and find the arbutus in bloom at last. The aroma of autumn would be gone, changed by winter's own alchemy into another kind of odor, fresh with spring yet still reminiscent of autumn and winter, a fragrance over which would rise the incomparable perfume of the trailing arbutus.

PERPETUATION

Spring? Not yet. Before spring could come, autumn must have completed its preparations for a long winter in order that life might be preserved to the next growing period. This mechanism of autumn is one of the most complex systems of the year. It must insure the carrying of life through the freezing period, the hungry period, the time of want and danger.

Perpetuation must have been simple enough in the days when there was no winter, when deciduous trees could lose their leaves and rest for a period, then, without that deadly interlude of cold, put out more leaves and grow again. Insects could follow through one generation after another in the usual way without requiring the life insurance of a dormant layover. Flowers could seed, and the seeds could sprout and grow without the interim of cold. It was a warm, simple, prolific world, uncomplicated by the rigors of a northern climate with its challenges and its triumphs.

The complications came about with the approach of that killer, winter, when it was necessary for plants and animals to survive in one way or another, so that they or their species might be alive in spring. The individual itself might not always live on; in itself it might perish—the butterfly, the poppy, the mushroom—but it must have been supplied with some winter-resistant means by which its descendants would carry on when winter was over. Species which could not manage this feat either became extinct or retreated to a less demanding habitat. The rest exhibited a multiplicity of means of survival, all of them good, all of them now proved to be successful. Because of the Ice Age and the seasonal changes which came after it, plants and animals, with splendid vigor, long since accomplished their own means of triumphing over winter.

Plants may be dormant, seeds put away, buds made, roots stocked with food, antifreeze solutions all in place, but unless insects also manage to survive the winter, the plants will not remain for long in the world. Therefore, nature has provided for the survival of the fragile yet obviously ironclad insects.

Because the earliest spring flowers come so quickly after winter that there could not possibly be time for insect eggs to hatch into larvae and the larvae to become adults in time to pollinate such flowers as Dutchman's-breeches, trout lilies, or hepaticas, nature provides that some fertilized females shall stay alive all winter. The big queen bumblebees often spend the winter well-sheltered under an old log. They are deeply embedded in the insulating decayed wood, and can thus emerge very early in the first mild days to perform their vital rite of visiting the earliest flowers. At the same time the bees nourish themselves on early nectar and gain strength for their own business of starting a new colony of bumblebees.

Among many insects there are four accepted patterns by which they may survive winter in the land the glaciers once knew. Butterflies embody all four methods of survival. Some—the swallowtails, spring azures, and American coppers—contrive to live as chrysalids through the winter, while others—the viceroy, pearl crescent, grayling, and the fritillaries, live as caterpillars in a sheltered place either of their own making or beneath a dried leaf or bit of bark. This hardiness seems incredible, considering the fragility of the caterpillar, yet some can evidently endure great cold.

Others manage to live through winter as adult butterflies. Even in Alaska and Labrador there are certain species which are sturdy enough to remain alive for months of cold and to revive in spring in order to go about the business of laying eggs.

On many a sunny winter day when a false but beautiful warmth steals into the bare woods and heats the bark of a maple or spruce, a butterfly may emerge. When I have walked in the woods at such

THE ALCHEMY OF AUTUMN

a time, discouraged with ever finding anything that looks alive, I have thrilled to see a butterfly! It may be a red admiral, an anglewing—either the violet tip or the hop merchant with its silver question mark on its wings—or the dark mourning cloak with its brown-black wings margined with a ragged border of pale yellow. Perhaps to me the mourning cloak is most exciting, most heraldic of spring long before true spring is near.

For a little while in the weak sunshine of February or March, the butterfly flits about on obviously creaking wing-joints, and then, with the coming of a cloud over the sun or the approach of the chill evening, it retires once more behind a piece of bark and becomes stiff and dormant. As I thought of these sturdy insects, my eye caught the erratic flight of dark wings margined with pale yellow, like the last rim of sunlight as night comes down. There was a mourning cloak ambling about in the cool October air. Perhaps the butterfly had already holed in for the winter, then had come out again briefly in the pleasant autumn days. To see it now, and to know that I might come back and find this same dark butterfly again when the maple sap was running and the snow was beginning to melt from the south slopes, was a heartening thing. On the wings of a butterfly, I bridged the great desert of winter.

Another way to survive in the north, if you are a butterfly, is simply to leave the country with the migrating birds. A few insects do just this, chiefly the monarch butterflies and some of the sulphurs. They have been doing so for thousands of years, perhaps at least since the close of the Ice Age, some of them traveling from Alaska to California or even farther south each autumn.

With many insects, such as damselflies and dragonflies, the adults all die long before winter, but their nymphs or larvae live down in the mud of pond or river or lake. The young of the cicada lives in the ground, where one species remains for fifteen to seventeen years, others for only two. Ants become dormant; so do many other insects. Still others leave their eggs to carry the race from one year to the next.

For insects, plants, and the lower animals, winter means change, curtailment, and either death or dormancy. It is not so simple for warm-blooded creatures which must adapt to searing cold and smaller food supplies. Yet the north country is amply equipped with both mammals and birds which, often for more than half of the year, must live in a stern environment. That they succeed in doing so, in surviving with considerable aplomb and with what appears to be a serene disregard for what to us is downright punishment and a peril, is one of the wonders of life in the presence of that annual glacier, winter. It is, at the same time, vital proof of how living things acquired, through the hardships of the Ice Age, the ability to remain in the north.

A great many of the birds simply clear out. Winter and cold are not for them. At the same time, in their departure, they reduce the pressure of competition for the existing food. These migrants are birds whose homes really are in the tropics, and they come north each year only for the nesting period because they find more space, more food, and greater elbowroom there to rear their young. With this accomplished, they fly south to their ancestral homes in Mexico and South America. They actually spend much more time there than here, yet we are accustomed to thinking of these Pan-American birds as solely ours.

In spring the flood of birds goes north with the northward-moving spring sun. They come into a land of new leaves and new insects, where long hours of daylight provide a plentiful time for feeding. The little warblers, flying north from the tropics to nest in the Boreal Zone, follow a burgeoning crop of canker worms and other small, leaf-eating insects which are making lacework of the new leaves. The birds pursue this flood of the leaf-worms from Louisiana to Alaska. By August many of the warblers, having nested, are on their way back south again. With them go many other species, all those with tropical affiliations. They leave behind them in the north only the birds whose food habits can adapt to the

THE ALCHEMY OF AUTUMN

supplies which are still available in the hungry period of the year. Those which remain are often joined by species which have come down from the still farther north. Cold does not seem to bother them. They simply move into more food-filled areas.

Most of the birds remaining all winter in our northern sections are the same as, or are closely akin to, the birds of northern Europe and Asia, particularly of the former. These are the winter-hardy ones—chickadees, kinglets, brown creepers, juncos, nuthatches, woodpeckers, jays, siskins, crossbills, evening grosbeaks—which evidently see no need to go elsewhere when winter comes.

The majority of these seldom show any apparent discomfort. They are warm inside as long as they have food. The body heat of a chickadee, for example, is about 110 degrees F., heat which is kept in by the dense, downy covering of the bird's tiny, vulnerable body. Further insulating it are the overlapping, coarser, outer feathers. Feathers are a perfect protection so long as the bird finds food for fuel. Nowhere, and in no matter what amount of freezing weather, have I ever come upon a really hungry-looking chicadee, or one which did not radiate well-being and satisfaction.

The winter birds must therefore use the available food supplies, must be either carnivorous, or seed- and fruit-eaters. The latter find food in weed patches, in pine cones and birch seeds, and in many other larders, in left-over holly berries, cedar berries, and high-bush cranberries. The carnivorous birds manage to find enough food— the chickadees and nuthatches eat insect eggs; the hawks and owls catch snowshoe hares and chickadees.

THE GAME OF MUSICAL CHAIRS

A great shifting of bird populations takes place in autumn and again in spring. There is not only the great flight to the south and back again, often nine months apart, as in the warblers, but a shifting even of the so-called permanent residents. In city areas this is sometimes more noticeable than in the wild. Your cardinal in the

Chickadee

winter garden may be the cardinal which nests in my garden next summer. The song sparrow from the park may live in my forsythia bushes all winter and visit my feeding places, while the Carolina wren which normally nests along the river bank five miles away may spend its winters in town. It is something like a game of musical chairs in which everything takes a somewhat different seat when the music changes—but not for long. Soon everything is getting up restlessly and shifting again as a different tune comes from the insistent pipes of the wild. Winter is the great reason for the major shifting—a moving about which often begins in August, only to begin again in January far down in South America. In February the northern horned larks and Lapland longspurs which wintered in Illinois stubble-fields are moving north with high-pitched twitterings in the sunshine. It is still a long, long way from spring, yet the larks and longspurs are heading for Saskatchewan. They are going home.

ANIMALS

Among the other creatures, I found preparations for winter taking place all along the way through autumn. Snapping turtles and painted turtles went down into the mud of the marsh. The bay was quiet and empty of life. Frogs had worked down into the ooze on the bottom. Their eyes had sunk into their heads; they had become inanimate, their hearts scarcely beating at all; yet they were not dead, only hibernating until spring. Of course I could not see this taking place here, but I had seen it happen in a laboratory—had seen the lively frog exercising furiously in warm water, then, as

THE ALCHEMY OF AUTUMN

ice was dropped in, growing sluggish and following that same procedure of passing into dormancy. A frog could not find food for itself in winter, would easily freeze to death out in the air. The only solution to its personal survival is for it to respond to its demands by slowing body processes and going gracefully into a state which almost, but not quite, is like death. Similarly, salamanders and snakes hibernate under logs and rocks, and in caverns. The skunks, woodchucks, most bears, and ground squirrels all follow the same example by crawling into burrows or caves to sleep the deep sleep of hibernation.

It is a slumber which is seldom broken until springtime. The hibernating animal has bent forward in a ball, so that both circulation and breathing are cramped and slowed. In close quarters, and in this position, the body processes grow more deliberate, metabolism ticks at a lower tempo, there is no excreta, little sign of heartbeat, only a very, very slight circulation of the blood. Yet the animals live, inanimate; it is their own way by which to outwit the winter.

Raccoons, muskrats, beavers—and some skunks, too, except in the extreme north—may sleep long hours, but they do not truly hibernate. They emerge frequently to find food. The chipmunks which we fed all summer with incredible quantities of peanuts, corn, prune seeds, and other delicacies (most of which were stored away in a winter den deep in the ground) sleep on top of their supply. When they awaken in winter they simply reach under themselves for a nourishing bite before sleeping again. The truly hibernating animal neither needs nor wakens for food.

In the north, squirrels and mice and shrews, rabbits and hares, foxes, bobcats, lynxes, deer, and porcupines all remain active and wide awake all winter, although many sleep longer hours because of the shorter hours of daylight. The problem of all, an ever present need, is to find food. Porcupines have an inexhaustible supply in the upper parts of aspens and pines whose tender bark they relish. In stormy weather, a porcupine may remain up in a tree, comfortable in a crotch, eating bark and sleeping there for days at a time before backing slowly down to drag big footprints through the snow to the next tree. The deer often are hard put to find adequate browse on the lower limbs and needles of arbor vitae and other favorite twigs which are within reach in the cedar swamps. Many starve unless game commissions bring hay and other food for them.

Squirrels spend their days in racing through the trees, challenging all comers, digging into the snow for cached seeds and nuts, chewing into cones for seeds, and otherwise providing very well for themselves. Because they are so active, they require much food. So must the tiny hunting shrew which is incessantly hungry for the blood and brains of small creatures, chiefly mice in winter. It pursues them relentlessly over the snow, or into the burrows which meadow mice have made in the depths. There the mice are safe from foxes, hawks, and owls which also are incessantly hungry and always hunting.

The rabbits and hares chew the bark of young trees, the canes of wild raspberry and blackberry. Somehow they survive—those which elude the hunger of fox and other meat-eaters. Whether they sleep all winter or hunt all winter, the mammals are arranged for, so that when spring comes they are all represented again, only lacking those which have served as necessary dinners for some of the others. The survivors set about the process of living and reproducing once more. This, after all, is the simple reason for all the complex autumn preparation.

THE ALCHEMY OF AUTUMN

Autumn—preparation—winter. The endless challenges and dramas of the north are what bring some of us back to it again and again, to where we find challenges for ourselves as well. The north seems to spur imagination and energy and invention. After all, man is one of the animals which had to adapt himself to winter weather and to the Ice Age's demands. His own ingenious mental growth in finding ways to be comfortable all winter has resulted in countless inventions, including modern heating and plumbing and lighting, food supplies, houses, clothing—as well as hot coffee, warm mittens, and fur coats borrowed from the wild.

This same ingenious north challenges me. It holds out its multiple questions and holds back many of the answers, making me seek them in cold bog and fragrant forest. Across the meadows and hills and rock ledges of today are the clues of the past. I will never find them all. But each walk, each exploration, each journey into a land influenced by the past and about to influence the future, brings me another short space toward the ultimate answers which may one day be revealed.

CHAPTER ELEVEN

THE ANATOMY OF NATURE

EVERYWHERE in the wild—in the mountain, in the bog, in the woods, in the lakes, on the sands—there were orderly arrangements of plants and animal habitats and successions. There were also repetitions of forms. These could not be accidental—not in terms of a calculating nature in which little is ever accidental. Similarities tantalized me—the oyster mushroom in the woods and the coral from the sea which looked so much like an oyster mushroom turned to stone, the sphere of earth and egg and cell and seed, the honeycomb in the beehive and the honeycomb of the coral in limestone, the star in the crinoid stem and the star in the apple.

When I began to search for these similarities, instead of just coming upon them by accident, I found the forms of life to be basically

THE ANATOMY OF NATURE

constructed of nine designs, or of modifications and combinations of those designs. Sometimes I found them in perfect, simple form, sometimes saw them united to use all nine, or again, employing only a few of them. I began to see the world as if through newly perceptive eyes.

These are the nine plans—the sphere and spheroid; the circle and ellipse; the cube; the cylinder; the spiral; the undulate; the pyramid and triangle, that composite of five triangles, the star or pentagon, and of six, the hexagon; the lattice; and the frond. I found that trying to identify the shapes of nature with these designs had become a fascinating game in which no landscape or object will ever appear monotonous or uninteresting. I also found a new philosophic and artistic venture into the strangely similar recurring designs of universe and man, of earth and animal, of all things that ever had their being or which will ever exist in the future.

Nature, far from being a diverse jumble of forms and things, shows plan and artistry and a nice assembling of designs into objects of incredibly varied character and beauty. I found the precision of geometry and the accuracy of mathematics, found line and form and pattern in ever more astounding numbers and repetition, down to infinitesimal details.

The spruce and balsam fir are a beautiful example of what can result when all nine forms of nature are put together to express one unit of life. Many more examples all prove the same theory, but these are outstandingly simple examples of a great and unifying truth.

The fir tree is a *pyramid*. Its root system and boughs are arranged in *fronds*, which spread outward from the great *cylinder* of the trunk. The branches *spiral* the trunk, and this is also the arrangement in the rows of scales on the flowers, in the cones, and in the way in which the needles are set around the twig. The outline of the tree is *undulate*. The resin ducts frequently are *cubes*; the needles, attenuated *cylinders*. Some of the wood fibers are *lattices*, and the cells in wood and needles are *spheres* or *spheroids*. The shadow of the tree makes a *circle* under it, but the lowering sun causes the fir or spruce to cast a long, *triangular* shadow. The whole combination is the tenth form, the *composite*, to make the complete tree in its grace, dignity, power, and strangely commanding beauty.

There is certainly nothing haphazard in this design. It is clearly expressed. I need not know its component parts, the botanical details of flowering and fruiting, or the lumberman's evaluation in terms of board feet and waste, to appreciate the tree. Nor do I require the wood-boring insect's one-track interest, the finch's preoccupation with its nest high in the tree, the viewpoint of the well-braced porcupine in a crotch. Nor do I need to know the origin of the scars on the trunk which a deer made when he polished the velvet from his antlers, or of the claw-marks left by a bear. I can appreciate the tree without knowing its name, although to many this is as essential to enjoyment as knowing the name of a friend. But the recognition of order, of seeing the beauty of form in a thing, stems from an awareness of the powerful, complicated simplicity of nature—nature which not only indicates in which habitat a plant or animal shall live, but combines forms with colors, textures, scents, and the miracle of life, to produce the creatures and landscapes of our world.

In *Nathan Coulter,* by Wendell Berry, the old man liked to wander about the country

"looking at the mountains and rivers and oceans that the Lord had made. Since the Lord had gone to all the trouble of making them, he thought the least a man could do was go and look at them."

I too feel that this is indeed the least that I can do.

"TRIANGLES ARE COMMANDS OF GOD"

Everywhere I find the plans and the designs. The triangle is the minimum of lines which may join to make a geometric figure supporting itself on all sides. The pyramid is the triangle given three dimensions, and the cone is the pyramid with all its angles smoothed to roundness. These three similar forms are part of the substance of some of the world's best natural designs. Two triangles laid together, points to bases, make a rectangle or a square, and when two are laid end to end, flat base to flat base, they make a diamond. Given three dimensions by using pyramids instead of triangles, they form crystals of many minerals. Six triangles, the points out and bases joining, make a six-pointed star; five make the five-pointed star. If a line is drawn to connect the points of the six-parted one, they are enclosed to make a hexagon. When the five-pointed star is connected, it makes a pentagon. Hexagons, stars, pentagons, squares, and triangles are basic forms of the greatest numbers of flowers in the world, just as the sphere and spheroid are the basic forms of seeds, pollen grains, and cells.

But before I explore pentagons and hexagons in nature, I cannot forget that simplicity of the triangle. While two crossed triangles make the orange Turk's-cap lily, one makes the blue spiderwort. The same shape forms the papaw flower, the wild ginger, the tiny pale-yellow blossom of the beach rush, the center of an iris. There are triangular diatoms, and triangular poplar leaves, and triangular fronds of the big bracken ferns, the small oak fern, beech fern, and rattlesnake fern. The long triangles wrapped around the trunk of the palm tree mark where the leaves once grew. There are triangular shark's teeth on a seashore, and three-pointed scales on a gar.

In the spring woods I find the trilliums counting by threes, not only in the flower itself, but in all the parts—leaves, petals, pistil, and seed pod. At times something happens to the trillium's counting, and it sounds off in fours. This is startling; it is also reassuring. When thrown off balance from the traditional triangular blueprint, a trillium still seems to follow a definite pattern. If there are four petals, then there are four sepals and four leaves, a four-parted pistil with four cavities in the pod. In its aberrations it is consistent, and in finding an example of this orderliness, I am assured of all the rest of that magnificent planning which is represented in the natural world.

JOURNEYS IN GREEN PLACES

Lilies, sedges and rushes, and, in strangely modified form, the orchids, follow the pattern of three. In the mustard family, in radish blossoms, rock cress, wallflowers, and in cranberry, snowberry, bluets, bedstraw, and partridgeberry, the parts are arranged in four to make, not a triangle, but a square. Fives are perhaps most abundantly represented in flowers—fives in roses, figworts, clovers, violets, geraniums, primroses, and chickweeds, and in many of the members of the more unreliable buttercup tribe. There is a considerable amount of experimentation in the latter group, which is believed to have been one of the first to evolve true flowers with petals in a world of petal-less plants. To this day, the buttercup family can't decide just how many petals to have, usually ranging from five to seven. Parts may be petal-like sepals, as in buttercups and anemones; or tubes, as in columbine; or spurs, as in larkspur; or without petals and only a great many stamens, as in baneberry. Nevertheless, in the majority of flowers, one of the greatest wonders in the out of doors is the very fact that they follow orderly plans based on geometry and arithmetic. But to express superlatives or generalities is dangerous—it must be borne in mind that in nature nothing can be taken for granted. When I expect flowers to conform to pre-ordained designs, I am then occasionally confounded in my self-assurance by a trillium which has become a quadrillium!

STARS

Five triangles make the star. In the world of nature, as in the world of man, the number five is a magical and often mystic figure, as old as the earth. It appears in some of the earth's most ancient life forms. It lies in the center of the crinoid segment that lived four hundred million years ago, and in the even older blastoid fossil called Pentramites, with its star-shaped top. It is in the delicate, five-fingered hands of a lizard, in the arms of the starfish, in the top of the sand dollar, in the star-anise seed, in the leaf of the sweet-gum tree—stars in the starch-cells of that calcium-bearing alga called chara, and in the earthstar mushroom. It is in all those five-parted flowers whose petals radiate from the center, in their five-plan calyces, their five-chambered seed pods—in all these, as well as in the apple.

To find that hidden star, cut an apple crosswise, half-way between stem-end and blossom-end. In cross section, the five seed chambers or carpels, with their oval seeds, form a perfect star. It is the symbolic pentagon of nature which recurs everywhere, often in unexpected places. We truly live in a star-studded world.

The star form was noticed and its mysteries deeply pondered by ancient philosophers and teachers. Pythagoras in Greece used the six-pointed star as a secret symbol for his followers in knowledge, the Society of the Star.

King Solomon's six-pointed figure became the mystic Solomon's Seal—two interlocking equilateral triangles, one dark, the other light, to symbolize the union of soul and body, like the Oriental yang and yin. This Solomon's Seal was used as an amulet to guard against fevers and disease. In our own woods grows the plant called Solomon's seal whose rootstock is marked with rough approximations of that ancient star-amulet design. It is also the pattern of the Jewish Star of David, and of the mysterious, extinct discoasters which lived in the world's oceans and died when the Ice Age began.

Stars are everywhere—five is everywhere. It was the number of some of the great movements and ideas of the world. There were the Five Blessings of the Chinese—long life, wealth, tranquility, love of virtue, and a peaceful end. There were the five Books of Moses, the Five Classics of Confucius, Napoleon's Five Codes, the Five Points of Calvinism, Russia's old Five-Year Plan, the Five Nations of the Iroquois, the Five Civilized Nations of the South.

But man only took his conception of five from nature, and in nature, wherever I look, the star meets my eyes. It is not only hidden inside the apple. It lies in the form of its flowers and at the blossom-end of the fruit when the petals have fallen. In all fruits and flowers of the rose family, surely more than any other number in flowers, it is represented faithfully and with precision. And nature, cunningly producing variations on the theme of the simple star, altered some to make the sweet-pea shape, changed others into tubes, as in the mints and figworts, yet retained the five divisions on the flower-opening. The composites elaborated on flower design by adding ray florets, yet the seed-producing flowers remain five-parted. The disk of a large sunflower may hold a whole galaxy of tiny, perfect, golden stars.

HEXAGON

What nature has contrived to do with triangles is a marvel to behold. When three triangles are arranged with the points inward, just touching, there is achieved only a loose form, a windmill effect which, with the least motion or revolution, may fly apart into space. It has no stability. But in filling the gaps with three lines, the loose triangles are at once connected to make six; and with this is created the wonderful hexagon. It is a six-sided figure of tremendous strength, versatility, and usefulness. It is one of the most efficient forms when arranging a quantity of units in a given area. There is no waste space; each side of each hexagon forms the side of another. The same effect is also achieved by placing a quantity of pliable spheres or circles just touching, and then exerting some pressure to squeeze them all closer together. The sides flatten, and—if the pressure is equal on all sides—the hexagons are produced.

It is a form which has been utilized in structures built by insects, bryozoans, and certain plant cells, as well as in the formation of snowflakes and the hexagon system of crystals. Quartz crystals are formed in this pattern; so are the secondary hexagonal prisms. Since quartz is called the most abundant crystal in the world—most sand grains are made of it—and snowflakes are another vastly abundant crystalline form, the hexagon and its many variations are surely one of the most frequent and favorite forms of nature.

It is admirably well suited to withstand pressure in colonial organisms in the sea, such as the corals. With six sides, pressure from seawater as well as from the surrounding members of the colony is equalized and crushing averted. The individual cell at the same time is strengthened by those around it. It cannot be crushed as the triangle, the square, or the circle might be, efficient though these forms are in many situations. The bees and wasps, in building colonial nests and combs, use the hexagonal form which has withstood not only the pressure of surrounding cells filled with liquid or with young grubs but the pressure of time and change. The hexagon for ages has been the efficient shape for honeycombs, for many corals, for wasp's-nests, for parenchyma cells in leaves, and as the unit of structure in the wonderful compound eye of the insect.

SPIRALS

The marvelous order of nature is seen clearly in the spiral. Growth in most plants is itself a spiral act. The shoot, when stopped-down to slow motion by delayed-action photography, may be seen to rise and extend itself in a sinuous movement, like the weaving back and forth of a snake's head and body. A vine which reaches out toward a support does not reach straight out, but describes a spiral. I can see this spiraling of branches up a tree trunk and in spruce needles arranged around the twig. The spiral is a deeply inculcated system in the conifers. Not only are the branches and needles so arranged, but the overlapping scales of pistillate and staminate flower cones also use it; and it materializes as the spiral arrangement of woody scales in the mature cone. A flexible wire secured around a cone to follow the rising spiral of scales becomes a coiled spring-wire, for the cone is no quiescent structure; it is a lively, climbing whorl.

Spirals are everywhere—by thousands in the birch trees in spring when the catkins are growing, for the scales of each one are arranged spirally. It is the same kind of form employed by the twining vine and its tendrils, in the curve of a lily's petal, in the snail's shell, in the eelgrass flower stem. It is an enormous, celestial form, as in a spiral nebula, or microscopic, as in the stalk of the protozoan, Vorticella.

UNDULATES

The undulate is like an unwound spiral, a rippling which stands erect or lies flat. It is in the waves on the summer shore, or the mark left by the spent wave itself as it meets the sand. It is as intangible as the flight of the bird which leaves no more mark on the air through which it has bounded than the sunfish has left an undulating imprint of movement in the water behind it. Yet it is as tangible as the frozen impression of wave action petrified on ancient beaches, solidified in the sandstone records of past waters. The wind, forever gnawing at the loose dunes, carves patterns in undulating curves. So also did the prehistoric waters of the Mississippi in the limestone cliffs of Illinois, to form a massive, undulating wall.

The wave breaks upon the shore, disperses, draws back, forms, crests, comes forward white-combed, and breaks again as waves have been breaking on shores ever since there were waters and winds and beaches, almost as long as the earth itself has existed. As the water draws back—on seashore, lake shore, pond shore, or in the mud puddle in the path—the wave leaves its mark, like an unwound spiral laid there. The same wave-line is plainly drawn on many sea shells and in their contours, as if they were ornamented thus to fit their environment. The trees on the horizon present an undulating line against the sky. So do clouds, the wind over wheat, the course of a river or a stream, the leap of a grasshopper, the grace of antelopes, the flight of bats—that same basic form which archaic waters imprinted on beaches long since turned to stone. It is the same pattern made by the snake in the dust, by the laurel bud's fluted contour, by the worm in the mud, or by the curve in the tail of the cat as it prowls in the mystic darkness of the summer night.

THE ANATOMY OF NATURE

FRONDS AND LATTICES

The frond is an ellipse, a circle, or a triangle which has been sliced into narrow sections almost to the center to make a feather or a fan. It is expressed most vividly in plants, perhaps, by the fern frond itself, in which the dissecting of the solid form reaches its most complex design and variation. It is also the form of the branching of coniferous trees, particularly of the fir and the arbor vitae. It is the fan-coral in the sea, the fantail of peacock, junco, and redstart, in the feather itself, the fan-arrangement of microscopic diatoms and protozoa, the frond-form of water courses in a delta, and the shape of the elm. Fronds may be palm leaves or ash leaves or leaf-veins or moth antennae. Fronds are in the growth of mycelium and roots, in the pattern of dendrites in rock, and in the frost on a window pane.

Lattices are much less common, most of them concealed within other structures. The lattice is often a supporting form—the arrangement of cells within stem or leaf, of the bones in a skeleton, of some coral colonies, of the spicules in sponges, and the way in which some tree-bark cracks with age.

Our own creations themselves seem to be limited in their fineness when compared with natural design. Under a microscope, the most beautiful craftsmanship becomes gross, the more so with the higher magnification to which it is submitted. But in nature nothing is coarse. The more it is magnified, the greater and more astounding is its beauty and infinitely fine detail. Perhaps this is one more great reason for seeking truths in nature, for while there are always great rewards and quantities of answers, there is never any end. Each thing in its visible form also has an invisible form which hand lens and microscope may uncover, yet only to the extent of their own power, and of ours, so that the infinite, hidden core and character may never truly be known by any man. He may think he has found the ultimate truth, the secret of life itself, may label it learnedly with the cryptic title DNA—but the deep, basic, magnificent secret of life and why and how it took its multitudes of forms, and how it holds to the traditional patterns down to an infinity of detail and smallness—shall we ever really know?

In attempting to see and understand the story of life in a year, and at the same time to see and understand a little more clearly the story of past and future, we live a more secure and assured daily life. In knowing the orderly passage of time and events in the natural world, I can find a reassurance of ultimate rightness and order in myself and in my fellow creatures. The inevitability of April must, by its very certainty, allay the dark fears of winter, bomb, or holocaust.

The orderliness of nature seems to stand out most clearly in a locality in which there are changing seasons of great contrast, as they are in the land once covered by the ice sheets. To live in the tropics would be its own remarkable experience, telling one part of the story of the world, but in a northern climate the sharp delineation of the seasons enables the year to fall into a pattern. Events at a particular moment in the northern year put a date on the natural calendar. We time our own lives by the timing of the natural year.

When in January the migrant bird sets off from South America and in June reaches the same tree in Canada in which it nested the year before, perhaps on the same day it arrived last year, the calendar has added another fact to its ordering of the world. When the arbutus blossoms at the time of its required hours of light in the day, just as it did last spring, or a thousand years ago, or a hundred thousand years ago, the ordering of life-processes remains comfortingly stable. When trees carry out the annual procedure of making and storing food and then, in autumn, sealing off the ends of leaf-stems so that the autumn winds may sweep them from the twigs, and when plants and animals are readied to survive through another winter, I recognize all over again the assurance of all life's continuity.

Perhaps it may seem hard to have to endure a winter when greenery is gone and the landscape presents only a relentless severity. Yet, although winter in the north may be uncomfortable, sometimes ugly, often extraordinarily cruel, it is always a challenge. In the rigors of winter in the north I can see more clearly, perhaps, the procedures which are an interlocking plan in my part of the world, can see and surely understand far more vividly than if I were tropic-bred, how it must have been long ago when the seasons became defined, when they changed as the Ice Age came on. Our annual drama of winter is a chance to relive in a small measure and understand in one small package some of the vast preliminaries of the Glacial Era. If my springtime comes a great deal sooner than the great springtime of the interglacial periods and the final melting of ice two miles thick, which stood mightily on top of where I live now, then I can be thankful to have the chance to observe a great drama telescoped into meaningful and recognizable form.

In watching the annual preparations in autumn, I can understand the winter. In knowing winter, I can the better appreciate spring. To know of the natural world by means of plant growth and bird song and snow crystal is not to escape from the civilized world's challenges and harassments, but, with perhaps a calmer and more ordered mind, to understand them a little better. To be able to recognize the small details of the year is to possess a special long-range insight into the greater span of centuries of millennia, an insight which may be a balm to the nerves and the source of a broader tolerance of both man and nature.

A day of snow should perhaps be the last place and time and condition to foster this, yet the feeling is there, for in the falling snow I can all the better begin to understand the natural world around me. It was for this season that the oil droplets were put into the insulated pine needles, that the wintergreen was waxed, that birches, maples, and wild cherries were given a great deal of antifreeze sugar. It is the reason why the cocoon of the Cecropia is so well built and warm, why the deer mouse built a roof on an old bird's-nest and filled the hollow with feathers and birch-bark curls, why all the warblers left the woods last summer, why juncoes from Canada have moved into my garden for the winter. Winter is the reason why the snowy owls and evening grosbeaks sometimes come south; the reason for the bulbs and roots and rhizomes in the frozen ground, from which will come next spring's flowers; the reason for the buds on the trees, the chrysalids in the bark; and the explanation of why a queen bumblebee is sleeping beneath an old log that is now almost covered in the falling snow. None of these things would be necessary or would take place if there had been no Ice Age, no winter.

The very facts of the snow itself add marvel to contemplation of the years and its preparations and completions of the cycles of life. It was mainly a superabundance of snow which built the glaciers of the Ice Age. Given enough of them, the power of splintery little snowflakes may build glaciers two miles thick and alter the course of life in the northern hemisphere.

Snowflakes begin when a layer of cold air meets clouds of water vapor in the sky. Freezing, the vapor forms clear, transparent, invisible crystals which are carried rapidly up and down in the atmosphere. They fall, they swirl, they surge upward on air currents, and in the mad convolutions of their dance they begin to hang together. One invisible crystal of infinite thinness may be a nucleus which attracts others around it, as if it were a magnet. This is not at all haphazard. If it were, then snowflakes would be shapeless blobs of loose frost. Instead, it is performed as with infinite geometric plan. Hundreds, or more than hundreds, of the minute ice flakes are required to form the facets of one snowflake, and no two are alike among the billions which are produced in one good-sized snowstorm. Those forming at a temperature of close to thirty-two degrees F. are large, wet, and loose; high-cloud, low-temperature flakes are small, dry, and compact; but they are all built to the geometric plan of six.

Their designs are among the most incredible and unmatched forms in creation. Snow would no doubt have been snow and have answered its purpose of slow release of moisture without assuring that each tiny flake follow the rule of six and be symmetrical and beautiful in all its parts. Yet, as if each one was a gem to be preserved alone and admired in its perfection, all those transient snowflakes follow the law of crystallization ordained for them.

Snowflakes have the regulation six points of the hexagon. The six rays are each set at an angle of sixty degrees to the next. When at times the rays are only three, then the angles are precisely twice sixty degrees. If one point of the flake has an ornament, then each point must have the same. If design-lines are drawn from the point of each tip toward the center, then they meet at a smaller hexagon drawn there, frequently with still smaller hexagons inside that, and others, smaller and smaller, to an infinity of design. When the crystals are sometimes columnar, some are shaped like an axle with a tiny wheel at either end, while others are simply cylinders. Yet, each little wheel is six-sided, and the column or cylinder also has six sides.

And so the snow begins to fall, to be swept on the downward air currents and borne to earth, the flakes to be piled upon each other until their individual forms are lost. When they are high in the clouds, the ice crystals are transparent. When snowflakes fall, they are white. This is because quantities of very tiny air bubbles were caught up in the texture of the forming crystals. The microscopic air spaces reflect and refract light, and the flakes appear white—white as gull feathers, white as birch bark. Snow is considered to be the whitest white there is; yet in shadow it appears to be blue or purple, and under the glow of the northern lights it may shine red or green or pink, for its crystals pick up color as well as light. So great is its light-holding power that to go out into a snow-covered night is to travel in a strange, self-lit world where there is no real darkness.

The snowy birch woods at night have almost the light of early morning. The white trunks, the white snow, and the night-blue sky, with its glittering stars snapping and seeming to shoot sparks of color in the cold, create a strange other-world unlike any other place or time of year. In the whole marvel of the snow, there is really no night.

A great stillness is unbroken by sounds of owl or fox. There is no wind, and the silent trees hold around themselves some aura of last summer's warmth. A small thing goes off in bounds like a dark feather, leaving little clumps of tracks—the deer mouse is foraging. But there is no sound—and the woods have a mysterious light which is from the snow and the birch trunks and the stars. No sound—and the place and the time could be part of any northern winter, now or yesterday or tomorrow.

One snowflake on my coat—it vanishes in a breath. Yet snow is still one of the natural giants which man, with all his mental and physical advances, has not yet learned wholly to master. We still have very little, if anything, to say about the vast tonnage of snow which is periodically dumped on New York or Chicago or Buffalo or, even more catastrophically, upon the south. Nor are we able, of our own volition, with the strength of body and brain, and unaided by the natural laws of the universe, to fashion a single snowflake. The thought is a humbling one, yet inspiring, too.

We occasionally need the primitive experience of a snowstorm to reduce our ego a trifle. We will take up the business-end of a snow shovel and set to work to dig a path from house to garage, from garage to street, and hope that the city crew will have been on the job to clear a way for us to drive to work—*if* the car will start. If not, and if the blizzard is a tremendous one, then we may even be snowed in. Power may be off. We may have to resort to candles and hearth for light and heat, and may have to cook dinner in the fireplace. As quickly as that, presented as monumentally as a major disaster and as innocently as a single fragile snowflake, well-ordered to the plan of six, we can be nicely cut down to size and reduced to a momentarily astonishing return to pioneer conditions. We are at the mercy of nature. As long as nature can still do that, perhaps man for a while longer is safe from himself. The laws of nature still must govern his own laws.

Those are the same laws which have shaped the woods and the bogs and the lakes and dunes, which regulate where each thing will grow, with order and reason and success, and which give deep significance to the potentials of the water, the sand, the sky, and a flying bird.

BIBLIOGRAPHY

Brown, William H., *The Plant Kingdom*, Ginn and Co., Boston, 1935.
Downing, Elliott R., *A Naturalist in the Great Lakes Region*, University of Chicago Press, 1924.
Fernald, Merritt Lyndon, *Gray's Manual of Botany*, 8th Ed., American Book Company, 1950.
Flint, Richard Foster, *Glacial Geology and the Pleistocene Epoch*, John Wiley and Sons, Inc., New York, 1948.
Gleason, Henry A., *New Britton and Brown, Illustrated Flora of Northeastern United States and Adjacent Canada*, New York Botanical Garden, 1952.
Hale, Mason E., *Lichen Handbook*, Smithsonian Institution, Washington, D.C., 1961.
Lobeck, Armin K., *Things Maps Don't Tell Us*, The Macmillan Company, New York, 1962.
Matthews, F. Schuyler, *Field Book of American Wildflowers*, G. P. Putnam's Sons, New York.
McCormick, Jack, *The Living Forest*, Harper and Bros., New York, with the American Museum of Natural History, 1959.
Morgan, Ann, Haven, *Field Book of Ponds and Streams*, G. P. Putnam's Sons, New York.
Niles, Grace G., *Bog Trotting for Orchids*, G. P. Putnam's Sons, New York, 1904.
Oosting, Henry J., *The Study of Plant Communities*, W. H. Freeman and Company, San Francisco, 1948.
Ward, Henry B., and Whipple, George C., *Fresh-water Biology*, John Wiley and Sons, Inc., New York, 1945.

INDEX

Adder's Tongue, *Erythronium americanum*, 147
Adventures with Orchids, 100
Alchemy of Autumn, 180
Alder, Speckled, *Alnus rugosa*, 134
Anatomy of Nature, 200
Andromeda, *Andromeda glaucophylla*, 80
Animals, 196
Ant Lion, *Myrmeleon*, 66
Ant Nests, 67-68, 96
Ant, Carpenter, 143, 160
Anti-freeze, Natural, 186
Arbor Vitae, *Thuja occidentalis*, 37, 39, 129
Arbutus, Trailing, *Epigaea repens*, 50
Arctic Ocean, 7, 8
Arethusa, 102
Aroma of Autumn, 180
Arrowhead, *Sagittaria*, 174
Aspen, Quaking, *Populus tremuloides*, 117, 181
Autumn, 180

Bailey's Harbor, Wis., 31
Balm of Gilead, *Populus balsamifera*, 37
Balsam Fir, *Abies balsamea*, 118
Baneberry, *Actaea alba* and *rubra*, 155
Barren Grounds, 59
Bear, 177
Bearberry, *Arctostaphylos Uva-ursi*, 69
Bee, 105
Bee-fly, 27
Beech, *Fagus americana*, 150

Beech Drops, *Epifagus virginiana*, 155
Birch, Canoe or Paper, *Betula papyrifera*, 117, 142, 149, 181
Birch, Yellow, *Betula lutea*, 117, 123
Birch Bark, 151-153
Birch Polyporous, 153
Bird Migration, 194
Birds, 194
Bird's Nest Mushroom, *Cyathus striatus*, 63
Bishop's Cap, *Mitella nuda*, 109
Bladderwort, *Utricularia*, 85, 87
Bloodroot, *Sanguinaria canadensis*, 146
Blue Haze, 188
Blueberry, *Vaccinium*, 50, 121
Bogs, 74, 85
Bog Trotting for Orchids, 101
Boreal Botany, 16
Boreal Zone, 15, 31
Bracken, *Pteridium Aquilinum*, 121, 181
Bryozoans, 179
Buckbean, *Menyanthes canadensis*, 73
Bumblebee, Queen, 192
Bunchberry, *Cornus canadensis*, 46, 121
Bur-reed, *Sparganium*, 174, 175
Burroughs, John, 129
Butterflies, 192
Butterwort, *Pinguicula vulgaris*, 90

Calla, Wild, *Calla palustris*, 96
Calopogon, 104, 113
Calypso, 108-110
Camas, White, *Zigadenus glaucus*, 71
Canadian Carpet, 44, 154

INDEX

Canadian Shield, 21
Cassandra, *Chamaedaphne calyculata*, 80, 96
Cedar Swamp, 133
Cedar, White, *Thuja occidentalis*, 37, 39, 129
Chara, 4, 22
Cherry, Bird, *Prunus pensylvanica*, 118
Cherry, Choke, *Prunus virginiana*, 118
Cherry, Sand, *Prunus pumila*, 24
Chickadee, 73
Chipmunk, 197
Cinquefoil, Silvery, *Potentilla anserina*, 24
Clintonia, *Clintonia borealis*, 49
Clubmoss, *Lycopodium*, 45
Colden, Jane, 133
Cladonia Lichen, 58, 59
Climax Forest, 117
Color, 183
Comandra, Northern, *Geocaulon lividus*, 71
Coniferous Forest, 115
Coral-root, Early, *Corallhoriza trifida*, 50
Coral-root, Striped, *Corallhoriza striata*, 50
Cranberry, *Vaccinium*, 97, 98
Cress, Sand, *Arabis lyrata*, 26
Cretaceous Period, 9

Darwin, Charles, 89, 90
Deciduous Woods, 136
Deer, 126, 178, 198
Deer Lick Ridges, 116
Discoasters, 9
Donacia Beetle, 163
Door County, Wisconsin, 3

Earthstars, 62

Fern, Cinnamon, *Osmunda cinnamomea*, 133, 134
Fir, Balsam, *Abies balsamea*, 118
Fire, 120
Fireweed, *Epilobium angustifolium*, 121
Floor of the Forest, 157
Flycatcher, Crested, 142

Forms of Nature, 201
Franklin, Sir John, 62
Frog, 197
Fronds and Lattices, 209
Fungi, 157

Garden Clubs of America, 33
Gaywings, *Polygala paucifolia*, 49
Gentian, Fringed, *Gentiana crinita*, 41
Glacial Era, 8
Glaciers, 10
Going Starring, 51
Goldthread, *Coptis trifolia*, 132
Grand Marais, Minnesota, 91
Grass, Marram, *Ammophila breviligulata*, 23
Grass, Rye, *Elymus canadensis*, 23
Grass of Parnassus, *Parnassia glauca*, 41, 44
Great Lakes, 15
Green Bay, 19
Grouse, Ruffed, 121

Haze, 188
Hemlock, *Tsuga canadensis*, 125
Heron, Great Blue, 176
Hexagon, 208
Hibernation, 197
Hornwort, Water, *Ceratophyllum demersum*, 167
Horsetail, *Equisetum scirpoides*, 43
Hunters, 26

Ice Age, 3, 8, 18, 74, 191
Indian Paintbrush, *Castilleja coccinea*, 38, 71
Indian Pipe, *Monotropa uniflora*, 155
Iris, Dwarf Lake, *Iris lacustris*, 68

Jay, Canada, 92
Juniper, *Juniperus horizontalis*, 38, 55

Labrador Tea, *Ledum groenlandicum*, 93
Ladies' Tresses, *Spiranthes*, 112
Lady's Slipper fertilization, 105
Lady's Slipper, Ram's Head, *Cyprepedium arietinum*, 50, 70

220

INDEX

Lady's Slipper, Showy, *Cyprepedium hirsutum*, 106, 108
Lady's Slipper, Yellow, *Cyprepedium Calceolus*, 107
Lake Huron, 18
Lake Michigan, 18
Lake Superior, 12, 90
Lamont Geological Laboratory, 8
Laurel, Bog, *Kalmia polifolia*, 94
Leatherleaf, *Chamaedaphne calyculata*, 80
Leaves, 156
Lichens, 58, 126
Light in the Forest, 155
Lighthouse, 31
Lily, Trout, *Erythronium americanum*, 147
Lily, Wood, *Lilium philadelphicum*, 38
Limestone, 5, 6, 141
Linnaeus, 152
Liverworts, 125, 159
Loon, 75
Luna Moth, 141

Maples, 116, 180
Maple syrup, 184
Marchantia liverwort, 159
Marl, 41
Migration, 194
Mistletoe, Dwarf, *Arceuthobium pusillum*, 56
Moccasin Flower, *Cyprepedium acaule*, 50, 108, 133
Mold, Slime, 159
Moosewood, *Acer pensylvanica*, 116
Mosquito, 84
Mosses, 125
Mouse, 152
Mushrooms, 122
Muskeg, 76

Nathan Coulter, 202
Niagara Escarpment, 18
Nicolet National Forest, 76
Nymphula Moth, 166

Oil in Plants, 185
Olson, Sigurd, 180

Orchids, 100
Orchis, Hooker's, *Habenaria Hookeri*, 111
Orchis, Purple-fringed, *Habenaria psychodes*, 38
Otter, 176
Our Wild Orchids, 101
Ovenbird, 149
Oxalis, *Oxalis montana*, 46

Partridge Berry, *Mitchella repens*, 47
Pea, Beach, *Lathyrus Japonica*, 24
Peninsula, Door, 18, 30
Pewee, Wood, 142
Philippine Islands Legend, 2
Perpetuation of Life, 191
Pickerel Weed, *Pontederia cordata*, 173
Pine Dunes, 54
Pine Ground, *Lycopodium*, 45
Pine, White, *Pinus Strobus*, 55, 116, 124
Pinguicula, 90
Pipsissewa, *Chimaphila maculata*, 51
Pitcher Plant, *Sarracenia purpurea*, 82, 84
Pliocene Era, 9
Polyphemus Moth, 141
Porcupine, 126
Preparation, 190
Primrose, Arctic, *Primula mistassinica*, 42

Quaking Bog, 85

Range Light, 31
Raspberry, Wild, *Rubus*, 121
Rattlesnake Plantain, *Goodyera repens*, 111
Reindeer Lichen, 58
Ridges, The, 30
Rock Tripe, 62
Rocket, Sea, *Cakile edentula*, 25
Roots of Spring, 146
Rosemary, Bog, *Andreomeda glaucophylla*, 80
Rush, Beach, *Juncus balticus var. littoralis*, 23

INDEX

St. John's Wort, Marsh, *Triadenum virginianum*, 171
Sand, 20, 29
Sawfly, 86
Searcher, Fiery, *Calosoma*, 26
Sedge, Bog, *Carex lasiocarpa*, 77
Sedge, Cottony, *Eriphorum*, 95
Service Berry, *Amelanchier laevis*, 118
Shrew, 161
Silurian Seas, 6
Skunk, 197
Skunk Cabbage, *Symplocarpus foetidus*, 145
Slime Mold, 159
Snail, 161
Snowflakes, 211
Snowberry, Creeping, *Gaultheria hispidula*, 48
Soil Fungi, 103
Sphagnum Moss, 77
Spider, Sand-colored, 27
Spirals, 207
Sponge, Fresh-water, 171
Spongilla Flies, 172
Spring Flowers, 146
Spruce, Black or Swamp, *Picea mariana*, 38, 39, 86, 87
Spruce, Engelmann, *Picea Engelmannii*, 119
Spruce, White, *Picea glauca*, 57
Squirrel, Red, 130, 131
Starflower, *Trientalis borealis*, 49
Stars, 204
Stump Gardens, 170
Subarctic, 86
Sugars, 184
Sundew, *Drosera rotundifolia*, 85, 88

Tamarack, *Larix decidua*, 39, 86, 119, 181
Tea, Labrador, *Ledum groenlandicum*, 93
Thimbleberry, *Rubus parviflorum*, 116

Thoreau quotes: *Morning air*, 187; *Pines*, 124; *Wilderness*, 37
Thrush, Hermit, 53, 128
Toft, Emma, 70
Tree Growth, 143, 144
Tree Nurseries, 130, 131
Trillium, White, *Trillium grandiflorum*, 150
Tundra, 14
Twinflower, *Linnaea borealis*, 51

Usnea Lichen, 58
Undulate Form, 208

Violet, Kidney-leaved, *Viola renifolia*, 126
Violet, Long-spurred, *Viola rostrata*, 140
Vireo Nest, 152

Washington, George, 62
Wasp, Digger, 27
Water Gardens, 162
Water Lily, White, *Nymphaea odorata*, 162, 164-165
Water Lily, Yellow, *Nuphar advena*, 165
Water Strider, 163
Went, Dr. Fritz, 189
Whirligig Beetles, 162
Winter, 191
Wintergreen, *Gaultheria procumbens*, 46
Wintergreen Ridge, 45
Witches' Brooms, 57
Wolf Lake, 76
Woodpeckers, 142
Wormwood, *Artemisia caudata*, 23
Wren, Winter, 126

Xanthoria Lichen, 61, 91

Zannichellia, 169